Library of
Davidson College

Medicine & Society
In America

Medicine & Society
In America

Advisory Editor

Charles E. Rosenberg
Professor of History
University of Pennsylvania

ON

THE CAUSES OF IDIOCY;

BEING

THE SUPPLEMENT TO A REPORT BY DR S. G. HOWE AND THE OTHER COMMISSIONERS APPOINTED BY THE GOVERNOR OF MASSACHUSETTS TO INQUIRE INTO THE CONDITION OF THE IDIOTS OF THE COMMONWEALTH, DATED FEBRUARY 26, 1848

WITH

AN APPENDIX

*A*RNO *P*RESS & *T*HE *N*EW *Y*ORK *T*IMES
New York   1972

Reprint Edition 1972 by Arno Press Inc.

Reprinted from a copy in
The Library of The College of
Physicians of Philadelphia

LC# 79-180578
ISBN 0-405-03955-7

Medicine and Society in America
ISBN for complete set: 0-405-03930-1
See last pages of this volume for titles.

Manufactured in the United States of America

ON

THE CAUSES OF IDIOCY;

BEING

THE SUPPLEMENT TO A REPORT BY DR S. G. HOWE AND THE OTHER COMMISSIONERS APPOINTED BY THE GOVERNOR OF MASSACHUSETTS TO INQUIRE INTO THE CONDITION OF THE IDIOTS OF THE COMMONWEALTH, DATED FEBRUARY 26, 1848.

WITH

AN APPENDIX.

EDINBURGH:
MACLACHLAN AND STEWART, SOUTH BRIDGE STREET.
LONDON: SIMPKIN, MARSHALL, AND CO.

MDCCCLVIII.

PRINTED BY NEILL AND COMPANY, EDINBURGH.

CONTENTS.

	Page
ON THE CAUSES OF IDIOCY. By Dr S. G. Howe and others,	1
The evils which now infest Society are not inevitable,	1
The prevalence of Idiocy indicates an extensive disregard, by Parents, of the natural conditions of the production of well-developed and healthy offspring,	2
Hereditary transmission of tendency to disease,	3
Definition and kinds of Idiocy,	6
Pure Idiots,	7
Fools,	10
Simpletons,	18
Circumstances or Causes which predispose persons to Idiocy,	23
The low condition of the Physical Organization of one or both Parents,	25
Intemperance,	28
Self-Abuse,	29
Intermarriage of Relatives,	33
Attempts to procure Abortion,	36
Conclusion,	37
GENERAL EXPLANATION OF THE TABLES,	39
TABLE I., showing the physical and mental condition of Idiotic persons in Massachusetts. (Reprinted in part.)	44
General Summary of Table I.:—	
A. Showing the actual measurement of Idiotic persons over 18 years of age, and their comparison with corresponding measurement of 1000 ordinary persons,	53
B. Showing the average of certain conditions of body and manifestations of mind in Idiotic persons, compared with similar conditions and manifestations in the average of ordinary persons,	53
C. Showing the actual development of certain parts of the Cranium in Idiotic persons; the average measurement of the same parts of the Cranium in 1000 ordinary persons; also the activity of certain mental manifestations in the same Idiots, compared with the average activity in ordinary persons,	54

CONTENTS.

	Page
TABLE II., showing the general condition and capacities of Idiotic persons examined,	55
TABLE III., showing the general *bodily* condition of the 574 Idiotic persons,	56
TABLE IV., showing the hereditary tendencies,	57
TABLE V., showing the physical condition of the 574 Idiotic persons,	58

APPENDIX.

No. I. Influence of the size of the Brain upon Idiocy. By Dr S. G. HOWE, ... 59

No. II. Results of the Experimental School for teaching and training Idiotic Children in Massachusetts. By Dr S. G. HOWE, . 65

No. III. Institution of the Massachusetts School for Idiotic and Feeble-minded Youth, 1850, ... 67

No. IV. Progress of the Massachusetts School for Idiotic and Feeble-minded Youth, to 1856. By Dr S. G. HOWE, . . . 68

No V. Relation of Poverty to Insanity and Idiocy. By Dr EDWARD JARVIS, ... 73

No. VI. Causes of Idiocy, reported by the Commissioners on Idiocy to the General Assembly of Connecticut, 1856, . . 77

No. VII. Schools in Great Britain for the Education of Idiots, . 79

INTRODUCTION.

THE Report, of which a portion is reprinted in the following pages, was drawn up by the Commissioners appointed under the authority of an act of the Legislature of Massachusetts, dated the 11th of April 1846, " to inquire into the condition of the idiots of the Commonwealth, to ascertain their number, and whether anything can be done in their behalf."

The Commissioners were Dr Samuel George Howe, Horatio Byington, and Gilman Kimball. The first of these gentlemen is extensively known in Europe as a zealous and accomplished educator of the blind. Ever ready to act when a great philanthropic object is in view, he took a deep interest in the inquiry, and lent his powerful aid in conducting the investigations, and in preparing the Report presented by the Commissioners to the Legislature.

In that instructive document they say:—" When we accepted the task assigned to us, it was not without a sense of its importance. We did not look upon idiocy as a thing which concerned only the hundred or thousand unfortunate creatures in this generation who are stunted or blighted by it; for even if means could be found of raising all the idiots now within our borders from their brutishness, and alleviating their suffering, the work would have to be done over again, because the next generation would be burdened with an equal number of them. Such means would only cut off the outward cancer, and leave the vicious sources of it in the system. We regarded idiocy as a disease of society; as an outward sign of an inward malady. It was hard to believe it to be in the order of Providence that the earth should always be cumbered with so many creatures in the human shape, but without the light of human reason. It seemed impious to attribute to the Creator any such glaring imperfection in his handy-work. It appeared to us certain that the existence of so many idiots in every generation *must* be the consequence of some violation of the *natural laws;*—that where there was so much suffering there must have been sin. We resolved, therefore, to seek for the *sources* of the evil, as well as to guage the depth and extent of the misery. It was to be expected that the search would oblige us to witness painful scenes, not only of misfortunes and sufferings, but of deformities and infirmities, the consequences of ignorance, vice, and depravity. The subjects of them, however, were brethren of the human family; the end proposed was not only to relieve their sufferings and improve their condition, but, if possible, to lessen such evils in coming generations; the task, therefore, was not to be shrunk from, however repulsive and painful was its contemplation.

"It is to be confessed, however, that we have been painfully disappointed by the sad reality; for the numbers of beings originally made in God's image, but now sunk in utter brutishness, is fearfully great, even beyond anything that had been anticipated.

"The examination of their physical condition forces one into scenes, from the contemplation of which the mind and the senses instinctively revolt.

"In searching for the causes of this wretchedness in the condition and habits of the progenitors of the sufferers, there is found a degree of physical deterioration, and of mental and moral darkness, which will hardly be credited.

"We would fain be spared any relation of what has been witnessed, as well for our own sake, as for the tastes and feelings of others, which must be shocked by the recital of it. It would be pleasanter simply to recommend such measures as would tend to remove the present evils and prevent their recurrence. But this may not be. Evils cannot be grappled with and overcome, unless their nature and extent are fully known. Besides, our duty was not only to examine into but to report upon the *condition* of the idiots in our Commonwealth; and that duty must be done.

"During the year 1846, we endeavoured, by means of circular letters addressed to the town-clerks, and to other persons in every town of the Commonwealth, to ascertain the number, and, as far as could be, the condition of the idiots in their respective neighbourhoods.

"The answers obtained to most of these inquiries were, in many cases, very vague and unsatisfactory. It was soon seen that little dependence could be placed upon information so obtained, even as to numbers, much less as to the condition and wants of the idiots. We therefore visited as many towns as possible, and endeavoured, by personal observation and by inquiries, to gather all the information in our power respecting the numbers and conditions and treatment of the unfortunate objects of our inquiry, both those in the public almshouses and at private charge.

"It was not possible, however, to obtain all the desired information, because the researches were begun too late in the season, and because the subject grew in importance and in dreadful interest, the more closely it was examined.

"The imperfect results of these inquiries were embodied in a report, made 15th March 1847, and printed by order of the legislature.

"Being directed to continue these labours, the painful inquiry was resumed during the last summer.

"By diligent and careful inquiries in nearly one hundred towns in different parts of the state, we have ascertained the existence and examined the condition of *five hundred and seventy-four* human beings who are condemned to hopeless idiocy, who are considered and treated as idiots by their neighbours, and left to their own brutishness. They are also idiotic in a legal sense; that is, they are regarded as incapable of entering into contracts, and are irresponsible for their actions, although some of them would not be considered as idiots according to the definition of idiocy by medical writers. There are a few cases where insanity has terminated in total *dementia*. There are others where the sufferers seemed to have had all their faculties in youth, and to have gradually lost them, not by insanity but unknown causes. Excluding such cases, there are four hundred and twenty persons who are to be regarded as truly idiots.

"These are found in 77 towns. But all these towns were not thoroughly examined. Take therefore only the 63 towns in which very minute inquiries were made. These contain an aggregate population of 185,942; among which were found 361 idiots, exclusive of insane persons. Now, if the other parts of the state contain the same proportion of idiots to their whole population, the total number in the Commonwealth is *between twelve and fifteen hundred!*"

"When attention was first turned to the subject, the number reported was supposed to be altogether an exaggeration; yet every succeeding examination has shown that the number is greater than that given by the preceding ones.

"Over four hundred idiots have been minutely inspected by us personally, or by an agent upon whom we can rely. Upon the bodily and mental condition of these will be based our remarks and conclusions.

"In an Appendix will be found their names,* ages, physical condition, and mental and moral character. It may seem to some, who inspect the tables, that they contain many trivial details with regard to the physical condition of the persons named; but it is hard to be too minute in these statements. The whole subject of idiocy is new. Science has not yet thrown her certain light upon its remote, or even its proximate causes. There is little doubt, however, that they are to be found in the CONDITION OF THE BODILY ORGANIZATION. The size and shape of the head, therefore; the proportionate development of its different parts; the condition of the nervous system; the temperament; the activity of the various functions; the development of the great cavities,—the chest and abdomen; the stature,—the weight,—every peculiarity, in short, that can be noted in a great number of individuals, may be valuable to future observers. We contribute our own observations to the store of facts, out of which science may, by and by, deduce general laws. If any bodily peculiarities, however minute, always accompany peculiar mental conditions, they become important; they are the finger-marks of the Creator, by which we learn to read his works.

"There are yet more subtle causes of idiocy existing in the bodily organization, and derived from the action

---

"* We have reported the names, as in duty bound, but would suggest and request that they be not printed, only referred to by numbers. The feelings and wishes of many worthy families would be thereby respected and gratified."

of that mysterious, but inevitable law, by which Nature, outraged in the persons of the parents, exacts her penalty from the persons of their children. We have endeavoured to throw some light upon this also; or rather to give a number of detached luminous points; trusting that more accurate observers will furnish many others, until all the dark surface shall be made bright, and the whole subject become clear.

" The tables have been made with great care; and though they cannot pretend to perfect accuracy, they are recommended to the physiologist and student of nature, as furnishing humble, but important data."

The Report contains a great deal of instructive matter in relation to the nature and treatment of idiocy, and the success which has rewarded the efforts of European educators to improve the condition of idiots. But to guard against misconception, it may be necessary to remind some readers that there are widely different *degrees* of idiocy. This is practically important, because if by an *idiot* be understood a person utterly devoid of sense and understanding, then idiocy is a very rare, instead of a very common state; and those who understand the word in this restricted sense, will naturally be predisposed to look upon all attempts to improve the condition of the idiot as visionary and impracticable. "Creatures," says the Report, " are sometimes born of woman, who are utterly wanting in the corporeal instruments by which understanding is most immediately manifested, —monsters without heads ; but Nature lets none such cumber the earth : they come into life only to die ; they take one short step from birth to death. All other beings in human shape manifest *some* sense and understanding."

Giving due weight to the facts collected, the Commissioners earnestly recommended " that measures be at once taken to rescue this most unfortunate class from the dreadful degradation in which they now grovel."

"The reasons for this," it is added, "are manifold, and hardly need to be repeated. In the first place, it would be an economical measure. This class of persons is always a burden upon the public. It is true, that the load is equally divided; it falls partly upon the treasury of the different towns, partly upon the state treasury, and partly upon individuals; so that the weight is not sensibly felt; but still it is not a whit the less heavy for that. There are at least a thousand persons of this class who not only contribute nothing to the common stock, but who are ravenous consumers; who are idle and often mischievous, and who are dead weights upon the material prosperity of the state. But this is not all; they are even worse than useless; they generally require a good deal of watching to prevent their doing mischief, and they occupy considerable part of the time of more industrious and valuable persons. Now it is made certain, by what has been done in other countries, that almost every one of these men and women, if not beyond middle age, may be made to observe all the decencies of life; to be tidy in their dress, cleanly in their habits, industrious at work, and even familiar with the simple elements of knowledge. If they were all made to earn something instead of spending, wasting, and destroying, the difference would be considerable. It would be an economy to some towns to send a young idiot across the ocean if he could be trained to such habits of industry as to support himself, instead of dragging out a life of two or three score years in the almshouse, and becoming every year more stupid, degraded, and disgusting. Many a town is now paying an extra price for the support of a drivelling idiot, who, if he had been properly trained, would be earning his own livelihood, under the care of discreet persons who would gladly board and clothe him for the sake of the work he could do.

"The moral evils resulting from the existence of a thousand and more of such persons in the community are still greater than the physical ones. The spectacle of human beings reduced to a state of brutishness, and given up to the indulgence of animal appetites and passions, is not only painful, but demoralizing in the last degree. Not only young children, but 'children of an older growth' are most injuriously affected by it. What virtuous parent could endure the thought of a beloved child living within the influence of an idiotic man or woman who knows none of the laws of conscience and morality, and none even of the requirements of decency? And yet, most of the idiots in our Commonwealth, unless absolutely caged up (as a few are), have, within their narrow range, some children who may mock them indeed, and tease them, but upon whom they in return inflict a more serious and lasting evil. Every such person is like a Upas tree, that poisons the whole moral atmosphere about him.

"But the immediate adoption of proper means for training and teaching idiots, may be urged upon higher grounds than that of expediency, or even of charity; it may be urged upon the ground of imperative duty. It has been shown, that the number of this wretched class is fearfully great; that a large part of them are directly at the public charge; that the whole of them are at the charge of the community in one way or another, because they cannot help themselves. It has been shown, that they are not only neglected, but that through ignorance they are so often badly treated and cruelly wronged, that, for want of proper means of training, some of them sink from mere weakness of mind into entire idiocy; so that, though born with a spark of intellect which might be nurtured into a flame, it is gradually extinguished, and they go down darkling to the grave, like the beasts that perish. Other countries are beginning to save such persons from their dreadful fate; and it must not be, that here, in the home of the Pilgrims, human beings, born with some sense, be allowed to sink into hopeless idiocy, for want of a helping hand.

" Massachusetts admits the right of all her citizens to a share in the blessings of education; she provides it liberally for all her more favoured children; if some be blind or deaf, she still continues to furnish them with special instruction at great cost; and will she longer neglect the poor idiot,—the most wretched of all who are born to her,—those who are usually abandoned by their fellows,—who can never, of themselves, step up upon the platform of humanity, will she leave them to their dreadful fate, to a life of brutishness, without an effort on their behalf?

" It is true, that the plea of ignorance can be made in excuse for the neglect and ill treatment which they have hitherto received; but this plea can avail us no longer. Other countries have shown us that idiots may be trained to habits of industry, cleanliness, and self-respect; that the highest of them may be measurably restored to self-control, and that the very lowest of them may be raised up from the slough of animal pollution in which they wallow; and can the men of other countries do more than we? Shall we, who can transmute granite and ice into gold and silver, and think it pleasant work,—shall we shrink from the higher task of transforming brutish men back into human shape? Other countries are beginning to rescue their idiots from further deterioration, and even to elevate them; and shall our commonwealth continue to bury the humble talent of lowly children committed to her motherly care, and let it rot in the earth, or shall she do all that can be done, to render it back with usury to Him who lent it? There should be no doubt about the answer to these questions. The humanity and justice of the legislature will prompt them to take immediate measures for the formation of a school or schools for the instruction and training of idiots.

"The benefits to be derived from the establishment of a school for this class of persons, upon humane and scientific principles, would be very great. Not only would all the idiots, who should be received into it, be improved in their bodily and mental condition, but all the others in the state and the country would be indirectly benefited. The school, if conducted by persons of skill and ability, would be a model for others. Valuable information would be disseminated through the country; it would be demonstrated that no idiot need be confined or restrained by force; that the young can be trained to industry, order, and self-respect; that they can be redeemed from odious and filthy habits, and that there is not one of any age, who may not be made more of a man, and less of a brute, by patience and kindness, directed by energy and skill.

"It is not our duty to enter into any details of the plan of such a school, or schools; that must be left to abler hands. We close this part of our Report, therefore, by most earnestly recommending, that immediate measures be taken for the formation of such a school. In the supplement will be found the result of our researches into the causes of the great frequency of idiocy in our borders, and such reflections as have been suggested by the examination of the subject generally. We have also prepared, with considerable labour, various tables in which is embodied a great deal of curious and interesting, if not valuable information."

This Report produced a great effect. Many persons became interested in the subject; and the Legislature, responding to the public sentiment, passed the following resolutions :—

"*Resolved*, That there be paid out of the treasury of the Commonwealth, a sum, not exceeding twenty-five hundred dollars annually, for the term of three years, for the purpose of training and teaching ten idiotic children, to be selected by the Governor and Council from those at public charge, or from the families of indigent persons in different parts of the Commonwealth, provided that an arrangement can be made by the Governor and Council with any suitable institution now patronized by the Commonwealth for charitable purposes; and provided that said appropriation shall not be made a charge upon the school fund.

"*Resolved*, That the trustees of the institution undertaking the instruction and training of said idiots, shall, at the end of each and every year, render to the Governor and Council an account of the actual expense incurred on account of said idiots; and if the amount expended shall be less than the sum received from the public treasury, the unexpended balance shall be deducted from the amount of the next annual appropriation.

"*Resolved*, That the said trustees shall be authorized to require that the authorities of any town which may send any idiot pauper to them for instruction, be required to keep them supplied with comfortable and decent clothing.

" Approved by the Governor, 8th May 1848."

Agreeably to the spirit of these resolutions, arrangements were made by the Governor with the Trustees of the Institution for the Blind to assume the responsibility for the proper expenditure of the money appropriated by the State; and from a Report made by Dr Howe to the Governor in February 1850, we learn that the work of instruction of thirteen idiots was begun in October 1848 by Mr James B. Richards, as teacher, and Mrs M'Donald as matron.

Notices of the further progress of this movement will be found in the Appendix.

It only remains to be added, that the present volume has been printed at the expense of the Trustees of the late William Ramsay Henderson, Esq., younger of Eildon Hall and Warriston, who in his settlement directed them to apply the residue of his property " in whatever manner they might judge best for the advancement and diffusion of the science of Phrenology, and the practical application thereof in particular." The Trustees are of opinion that the facts disclosed in this Report illustrate, in an impressive manner, the influence of the condition of the brain on the mental manifestations, and show the necessity of instructing all classes of the people in the functions of that organ, and in the circumstances which promote and impede its healthy development and activity, on which so much of human happiness depends. It appears to them, that such lessons as this Report affords are well calculated to rouse attention to the great expediency of introducing Physiology and the Laws of Health as a branch of general education into schools; and it is by this belief, as well as by the hope of promoting the improved treatment of our idiots, and helping to diminish the number of such unhappy persons in future, that they have been induced to undertake the present publication.

ON THE CAUSES OF IDIOCY.

THE object of the first part of this report was to lay before the proper authorities such information respecting the number and condition of idiots in the Commonwealth as would show the necessity for some immediate action in their behalf. In this supplementary part will be found some information which, perhaps, may be useful for those who shall have the direction of that action; and likewise some facts and considerations, the knowledge of which may tend to lessen the number of idiots in the next generation, and possibly to hasten the period at which the grievous calamity shall be removed.

All those who have a living and abiding faith and trust in the goodness and wisdom of the Creator will readily believe that the terrible evils which now infest society are not necessarily perpetual; that they are not inherent in the very constitution of man, but are the chastisements sent by a loving Father to bring back his children to obedience to his beneficent laws. These laws have been as much shrouded in darkness, in times past, as the hieroglyphics of Egypt; and though they were written upon every man's body, no Champollion was found to decipher them. But a better day has dawned, and men are beginning to read the handwriting upon the world, which tells them that every sin against a natural law must be atoned for by suffering *here* as well as hereafter.

It is beginning to be seen, also, that man has a double nature and double interests; that he is a social being, as well as an individual; and that he cannot sin with impunity against the one nature any more than he can against the other. God has joined men together, and they cannot put themselves asunder. The ignorance, the depravity, the sufferings of one man, or of one class of men, must affect other men, and other classes of men, in spite of all the barriers of pride and selfishness which they may erect around themselves. The doctrine of impenetrability does not obtain in morals, however it may do in physics; but, on the contrary, as gases afford mutually a vacuum to each other into which they rush, so the nature of every individual is a vacuum to the nature of society, and its influences, be they for good or be they for evil, interpenetrate him in spite of himself. It is clear, therefore, that in this, as in everything else, the interest and the duty of society are common and inseparable.

Idiocy is a fact in our history of momentous import. It is one of the many proofs of the immense space through which society has yet to advance before it even approaches to the perfection of civilization which is attainable. Idiots form one rank of that fearful host which is ever pressing upon society with its suffering, its miseries, and its crimes, and which society is ever trying to hold off at arm's length,—to keep in quarantine, to shut up in jails and almshouses, or, at least, to treat as a pariah caste; but all in vain.

There are the paupers,—a host in themselves; the drunkards, the vagabonds, the criminals, the insane, the blind, the deaf, —all these together form a number, the proportion of which to the whole population is fearfully great, and the existence of which is a reproach to our civilization, for that existence implies gross ignorance and open violation of the laws of nature.

The moral to be drawn from the existence of the individual idiot is this,—he, or his parents, have so far violated the natural laws, so far marred the beautiful organism of the body, that it is an unfit instrument for the manifestation of the powers of the soul. The moral to be drawn from the prevalent existence of idiocy in society is, that a very large class of persons ignore the conditions upon which alone health and reason are given to men, and consequently they sin in various ways; they disregard the conditions which should be observed in intermarriage; they overlook the hereditary transmission of certain morbid tendencies, or they pervert the natural appetites of the body into lusts of divers kinds,—the natural emotions of the mind into fearful passions,—and thus bring down the awful consequences of their own ignorance and sin upon the heads of their unoffending children.

Idiocy is found in all civilized countries, but it is not an evil necessarily inherent in society; it is not an accident; and much less is it a special dispensation of Providence; to suppose it can be so, is an insult to the Majesty of Heaven. No! It is merely the result of a violation of natural laws, which are simple, clear, and beautiful; which require only to be seen and known, in order to be loved; and which, if strictly observed for two or three generations, would totally remove from any family, however strongly predisposed to insanity or idiocy, all possibility of its recurrence.

No scientific exposition of these laws will be attempted here; but many facts and observations will be recorded, which may awaken some abler minds to the importance of codifying them and setting them forth for the benefit of mankind. Suffice it to say now, that out of 420 cases of congenital idiocy examined, some information was obtained respecting the condition of the progenitors of 359. Now, in all these 359 cases, *save only four*, it is found that one or the other, or both, of the immediate progenitors of the unfortunate sufferers had, in some way, widely departed from the normal condition of health, and violated the natural laws. That is to say, one or the other, or both of them, were very unhealthy or scrofulous; or they were hereditarily predisposed to affections of the brain, causing occasional insanity; or they had intermarried with blood relatives; or they had been intemperate, or had been guilty of sensual excesses which impaired their constitutions.

Now, it is reasonable to suppose, that if more accurate information could have been obtained about the history of the other four cases, some adequate cause would have been found in them also, for the misfortune of the child, in the condition of the progenitors.

This subject of the hereditary transmission of diseased tendency is of vast importance; but it is a difficult one to treat, because a squeamish delicacy makes people avoid it; but if ever the race is to be relieved of a tithe of the bodily ills which flesh is now heir to, it must be by a clear understanding of, and a willing obedience to, the law which makes the parents the blessing or the curse of the children; the givers of strength, and vigour, and beauty, or the dispensers of debility, and disease, and deformity. It is by the lever of enlightened parental love, more than by any other power, that mankind is to be raised to the highest attainable point of bodily perfection.

Can there be so sad a sight on earth as that of a parent looking upon a son deformed, or halt, or blind, or deaf, with the consciousness that he himself is the author of the infirmity; or upon a sick and suffering daughter, fading and dying in early youth, from the gnawing of a worm which he himself placed within her breast; or a wayward and unmanageable child, urged and hurried on to lust, and licentiousness, and crime, by the irresistible force of passions which he himself bestowed upon it? If such parent erred in ignorance; if he had always obeyed the laws of life and morality, as far as he knew them, still must his suffering be grievous; but if he sinned against the clear light of God's law; if he secretly defiled the temple of his soul, ran riot in lust, fed the fire of passion until it burnt out the very core of his body, and then planted a spark from the smouldering ashes to shoot up into unhallowed flames in the bosom of his child,—how horrible must be his sensations when he looks upon that child, consuming, morally, every day before his eyes! Talk about the dread of a material hell in the far-off future! The fear of that can be nothing to the fear of plunging one's own child in the hell of passion *here*. It is probable that there are thousands of such parents among us, who never dream that they are at all responsible for those bodily ailments of their offspring, which sadden their own lives; or for the stupidity, the waywardness, or the vice, which almost hardens their hearts against the children who manifest them, while, in reality, those ailments and vices are but the dregs of a poisoned chalice returned to their own lips.

It may be assumed as certain, that in all cases where children are born deformed, or blind, or deaf, or idiotic, or so imperfectly and feebly organized that they cannot come to maturity under ordinary circumstances, or have the seeds of early decay, or have original impetuosity of passions that amount to moral insanity,—in all such cases the fault lies with the progenitors. Whether they sinned in ignorance or in wilfulness, matters not as to the effect of the sin upon the offspring. The laws of God are so clear that he who *will* read may do so. If a man violates them ignorantly, he suffers the simple penalty; if he violates them knowingly, he has remorse added to his suffering ; but in no case can the penalty be remitted to him.

The conditions of the law of transmission of hereditary tendencies to disease of body and of mind are beginning to be known, but there are many circumstances which obstruct the spread of knowledge upon the subject. First and foremost among these is the mournful ignorance about Physiology. People are blind to principles which, if understood, would make the whole law clear and beautiful.

The transmission of any infirmity is not always direct. It is not always in the same form. It may be modified by the influence of one sound parent; it may skip a generation; it may affect one child more, and another less; it may affect one in one form and another in another ; and so, in a thousand ways, it may elude observation. But more especially does it escape observation, because it may affect a child merely by *diminishing*, not destroying, the vigour of his mind or body,— by almost paralyzing one mental faculty, or giving fearful activity to one animal passion, and so reappearing in the child, in a different dress from what it wore in the parent. Variety is the great law of nature, and it holds good in the transmission of diseased tendencies, as well as in everything else. But unerring certainty, too, is alike a characteristic of this law ; and let no one flatter himself or herself that its penalties can be escaped.

The health and vigour of the body may be compared to a man's capital; it is a trust fund given to him by the Creator, of which he may expend the interest in the natural enjoyments of life, but he cannot encroach in the least on the principal without real loss. Every debauch, every excess, every undue indulgence, is at the expense of this capital. A rich man may throw away cents or dollars, and not feel it,—but he is really poorer for it ; and a young man, with a large capital of health, may daily throw away part of it, and still feel strong ; but every over-stimulant to the nerves, every overload to the stomach, is a cent or a dollar taken from his capital ; feel it, or not feel it, he is poorer for it, and so will be the children afterwards born to him.

There is this difference, however, between the capital which God gives man, and that which he accumulates for himself, that the one is never so great but its interest can be spent with enjoyment, while the other may be so enormous as to cumber and embarrass him like an overload of fat. He may grasp so much, that, like the boy with his fist full of olives in the narrow-mouthed jar, he cannot withdraw it, and will not let any drop.

Were it not for the action of certain principles which give to the race recuperative powers, there would be danger of its utter deterioration as a whole by the sins of so many of its individual members.

The conviction of the existence and the importance of the law of hereditary influences has been brought home so strongly by examining the condition of the unfortunate objects of this research, that this digression has been inevitable.

Before referring to the tabular views appended, we shall attempt to give an idea of the leading differences among the persons referred to, although it is no part of the object of this report to establish a scientific classification of idiots. The best way, perhaps, to give an idea of the leading distinctive features of different classes of these unfortunate beings will be to describe several individual cases. For all humane and practical purposes, we may divide them into PURE IDIOTS, FOOLS, AND SIMPLETONS, or IMBECILES, as they are sometimes called.

According to Mr Séguin, the type of an idiot is an individual who "*knows nothing, can do nothing, cannot even desire to do anything.*" This is the maximum of idiocy; the minimum of intelligence; and but very few cases can be found (we were inclined to think none could) in which a being in human shape is so much below even insects, and so little above a sensitive plant. The vast European hospitals, in which the two ends of humanity seem to meet, where beneficence, guided by science, stoops to give attention to the most shocking and repulsive forms of human suffering and degradation;—those great lazar-houses of London and Paris do, sometimes, as their records show, present such cases of idiocy as, one would fain hope, can be found nowhere else. But, alas! when, overcoming the repugnance to close contemplation of utter degradation, one looks carefully among the *sweepings* that are cast out by society for something that may be saved to humanity, he finds, even in our fair commonwealth, breathing masses of flesh, fashioned in the shape of men, but shorn of all other human attributes.

IDIOTS OF THE LOWEST CLASS ARE MERE ORGANISMS, MASSES OF FLESH AND BONE IN HUMAN SHAPE, IN WHICH THE BRAIN AND NERVOUS SYSTEM HAS NO COMMAND OVER THE SYSTEM OF VOLUNTARY MUSCLES; AND WHICH CONSEQUENTLY ARE WITHOUT POWER OF LOCOMOTION, WITHOUT SPEECH, WITHOUT ANY MANIFESTATION OF INTELLECTUAL OR AFFECTIVE FACULTIES.

FOOLS ARE A HIGHER CLASS OF IDIOTS, IN WHOM THE BRAIN AND NERVOUS SYSTEM ARE SO FAR DEVELOPED AS TO GIVE PARTIAL COMMAND OF THE VOLUNTARY MUSCLES; WHO HAVE CONSEQUENTLY CONSIDERABLE POWER OF LOCOMOTION AND ANIMAL ACTION; PARTIAL DEVELOPMENT OF THE AFFECTIVE AND INTELLECTUAL FACULTIES, BUT ONLY THE FAINTEST GLIMMER OF REASON, AND VERY IMPERFECT SPEECH.

SIMPLETONS ARE THE HIGHEST CLASS OF IDIOTS, IN WHOM THE HARMONY BETWEEN THE NERVOUS AND MUSCULAR SYSTEM IS NEARLY PERFECT; WHO CONSEQUENTLY HAVE NORMAL POWERS OF LOCOMOTION AND ANIMAL ACTION; CONSIDERABLE ACTIVITY OF THE PERCEPTIVE AND AFFECTIVE FACULTIES; AND REASON ENOUGH FOR THEIR SIMPLE INDIVIDUAL GUIDANCE, BUT NOT ENOUGH FOR THEIR SOCIAL RELATIONS.

Among idiots proper should be classed the following cases:—

No. 410. E. G., aged 8 years. This poor creature may be taken as a type of the lowest kind of idiocy. He has bones, flesh, and muscles, body and limbs, skin, hair, &c. He is, in form and outline, like a human being, but in nothing else. Understanding he has none; and his only *sense* is that which leads him to contract the muscles of his throat, and swallow food when it is put into his mouth. He cannot chew his victuals; he cannot stand erect; he cannot even roll over when laid upon a rug; he cannot direct his hands enough to brush off the flies from his face; he has no language—none whatever; he cannot even make known his hunger, except by uneasy motions of his body. His habits of body are those of an infant just born. He makes a noise like that of a very sick and feeble baby, not crying, however, in a natural way. His head is not flattened and deformed, as is usual with idiots, but is of good size and proportion.

It would seem as if the powers of *innervation* were totally wanting in him. There is no nervous energy; nothing to brace the muscles; no more power of *contractility* than in a person who is dead drunk. The involuntary muscular motions are properly performed; that is, the organic life goes on regularly; the heart contracts and dilates; the peristaltic motion of the bowels is regular.

The probable causes are hereditary ones. The grand-parents were very scrofulous and unhealthy. The parents were apparently healthy, but gave themselves up to excessive sensual indulgence. They lost their health in consequence of this, and were so well aware of it as to abstain and to recover again. In the meantime, five children were born to them—two of whom were like E. G., and died at five or six years of age: two others were very feeble and puny, and died young.

No. 370. Male, aged 9 years. This organism in the human form is hardly a grade higher than the preceding. He has no muscular contractility; he cannot stand, nor sit upright, nor even turn over; for, if laid upon his stomach, he paws and kicks until turned over upon his back, which position he likes best. He has not even power to masticate his food, though he swallows very well when it is thrust into his mouth. He has no language, but seems to understand some simple sentences. He has more intelligence than the boy above named, and the principal trouble seems to be want of contractility. He can feel flies that alight upon his skin, and can brush them off. His habits are like those of an infant. His head is very small.

The causes are probably hereditary, and he seems to be the last and lowest of a constantly degenerating breed. The grand-parents were intemperate and depraved. The children born unto them were puny and weak-minded, and they sank still lower in the slough of vice and depravity. The mother of this boy was herself a simpleton; and this was her second illegitimate child. Though of feeble health, she gave herself up to excessive licentiousness, her passions becoming almost maniacal.

No. 325. H. W., aged 17. This wretched being seems to

be, like the preceding ones, so deficient in nervous energy that he lies almost as powerless as though he were a mass of jelly, without a bone or a muscle in his composition. If his legs are pinched or irritated, he seems to try to move them, but scarcely draws them up an inch. If flies alight upon his face, he can hardly reach them with his hand. He sometimes rolls his head from side to side with a languid motion, and this is the most he can do in that way, for he cannot raise it up even to take food. He is fed like a sick infant, with half-chewed victuals, from a spoon. He has no speech, and apparently no knowledge of persons. When food is brought near to him, something like a smile comes over his countenance; perhaps he is made aware of it by the smell.

His head is not very small, nor is it deformed. The family of which he comes is very scrofulous and degenerate physically. His relatives (especially his mother) are, many of them, remarkable for erysipelatous humours, tumours, carbuncles, &c. One of his cousins is idiotic, though not of so low a degree as he is.

It is remarkable, that in this case, as well as the two preceding, there is not the peculiar *look* so common with idiots, and which may be better expressed by the word *monkeyish* than any other. When the animal nature is pretty active, and there is, at the same time, a governing intellect, the resulting expression is human. The higher the intellectual endowment, the more lofty and noble is the look; the lower the degree of endowment, the more nearly the look approaches that of animals, until we get down to the mere twinkle of cunning in the low rogue or the monkeyish looks of the idiot.

Now, the three persons above mentioned do not seem to be idiotic from any deficiency in the size, or deformity in the shape or structure, of that part of the organization on which the manifestation of intelligence immediately depends. There is, at any rate, no appearance of anything of that kind; but there seems to be a want of *power* in that part of the organization by which the nervous fluid gives energetic action to the frame. The look is that of languor rather than that of idiocy.

Among idiots of the lowest class are found some who, unlike the preceding, seem to have a superabundance of *innervation*, who have great *muscular contractility*, that is, great command of all the muscles by the nervous system, and who are consequently very active. They appear like insane persons in a state of excitement, and yet they have no speech, and no reasoning faculties. The distinction made with so much ingenuity by a celebrated French writer holds true here,—"*The insane man reasons falsely, the idiot reasons not at all.*"

No. 35. Jonas ——, aged 8 years. His body is well-proportioned and strong, but very small. Face has the deformed look of idiocy. The sides of his head seem to be at a fever heat. He is almost all the time in violent motion. His appetite is not only voracious, but evidently morbid and insatiable; for, after eating heartily at table, he swallows anything he can lay his hands upon, raw potatoes, the bark of trees, chips of wood, and even small stones. He has been known to swallow pebbles as large as chestnuts. He hears and seems to understand the meaning of some sounds, but has no speech. He has no sense of propriety, no affection, no attachment; his brothers and sisters are no more to him than the dog and cat.

His father was intemperate to the last degree. His mother was of a very scrofulous habit of body.

Cases of this kind are not very frequent, and they are often mistaken for cases of insanity. They are generally proper subjects for instruction, though the long continuance of their life is not probable, for there seems to be morbid action in the brain.

FOOLS

MAKE THAT CLASS OF IDIOTS WHO HAVE THE MUSCULAR AND NERVOUS SYSTEM WELL DEVELOPED; POWERS OF LOCOMOTION AND ANIMAL ACTION; IMPERFECT SPEECH; PARTIAL DEVELOPMENT OF THE PERCEPTIVE AND AFFECTIVE FACULTIES, BUT VERY FEEBLE POWERS OF REASON.

This class is more numerous than the preceding. Cases are found in every town, in almost every almshouse. The type of this class would be a man who uses all his senses; who observes things about him; who can make simple sentences, and understand simple directions; but who obeys every animal impulse without any thought about responsibility to others, or consequences to himself.

The description of some of these cases will be put in such a form as to give an idea of the course that was followed in inquiring into the condition of these unfortunate persons.

It was obviously necessary to have some regular series of questions, or rather a series of subjects about which questions were framed upon the spot, and put in such form as the occasion and circumstances demanded.

Some of the terms used, as will be seen, are borrowed from a system of mental philosophy, which (however undeniable its claims are to have presented the clearest and best analysis of the human faculties ever yet known), has not been relied upon by the Commissioners in their examination. In speaking of the instinct to oppose and destroy, of the sentiment of self-esteem and love of approbation, the faculty of number, &c., as manifested in the following cases, no reference is had to the question whether there is or is not a proportionate development of those parts of the brain which some able anatomists and keen observers of nature maintain to be the part of the organization which is most immediately instrumental in the manifestion of such instinct, sentiment, or faculty. Indeed, in most cases, the notes were taken before the actual measurements were made. It was thought, however, that the close personal examination of so many idiots presented too rare and important an opportunity for ascertaining their craniological as well as other bodily peculiarities to be lost; and accordingly it was improved, and the general results may be found in the Tables. It may be stated here, in general terms, that the result of this examination and measurement shows that no dimensions of the head, except extreme diminutiveness, and no shape whatever, can be relied upon as criteria of idiocy. A few of the worst cases of idiocy are those in which the head is normal as to size and shape. Nevertheless, the Tables show that, taking the aggregate of all the cases, an obvious relation is seen between the size and development of the cranium, and of its different parts, and the amount of intellectual power, and of the different kinds of mental manifestation.

The results of the observations and measurements are published without any inference being drawn, in order that those who choose to examine and study them may do so.

Some writers have hastily concluded, that because a few idiots, whose heads were smaller than the measure which had been laid down as the *minimum* of brain by which intelligence could be manifested, have nevertheless been partially educated, and because many others, with heads of normal size and shape, are hopelessly idiotic, therefore the doctrine of the dependence of mental manifestation upon the structural condition of the brain is overthrown. They say, it has been asserted that persons with heads of a certain size must necessarily remain idiots, and they triumphantly point to certain idiots who have recently been trained to show a certain amount of intelligence, though their heads were smaller than this arbitrary standard.

This conclusion, however, does not seem justified by close and candid observation. *Size* is only *one* of the structural conditions of the brain upon which mental manifestations depend; —*quality* of fibre, health, exercise, &c., are others essentially modifying it. It may very well be that one anatomist and philosopher, who wrote fifty years ago, saying that a man with a head below a certain measurement must necessarily remain an idiot in spite of any means of education *then known*, would be still right in his general conclusions, notwithstanding means are *now* discovered to educe considerable intelligence out of such a supposed idiot. The result of close and extensive observations of idiots has been strongly to confirm, not only the doctrine of the *volume* of brain being one important element in the means of manifesting mental power, but all the main doctrines of that school of philosophy which teaches that God gives us the body not merely as the handmaid of the soul, but weds and welds the two together in bonds of dependence that death alone can sever.

That philosophy has been aptly illustrated by comparing the body to a musical instrument, the soul to an invisible player. It is indeed so; and if the harp have a thousand strings, and they all be kept in tune, then the soul discourses sweet and varied music. But the idiot's body is a wretched thing, and its few strings are so sadly awry, that even in a seraph's hand it could give nothing but jarring and discordant sounds.

The whole of the success which has recently been gained, in attempts to improve the condition of idiots, has arisen from the adoption in practice of the principles of that much-ridiculed doctrine which teaches that the first thing to be done is to put the *instrument* in tune. Surely, then, the attempt to show what are the material conditions of the bodily instrument in such a number of idiots as have been examined by the Commissioners will not be condemned by candid observers, as such attempts made upon other classes of men have too frequently been.

That the different degrees of keenness and vigour with which different *manifestations* of mind can be made by different individuals, and by the same individual at different times, do, in some way, depend upon the original nature and the actual condition of *some part* of the bodily organization,—none are now found foolish enough to deny; that they do depend, moreover, most immediately upon the structure and condition of the brain and nervous system, few will doubt; that there must be some peculiar corresponding outward signs by which the internal structure and condition of the brain and nervous system *may* be known by examination of the outward man, will not be questioned by sagacious observers of nature; that such examination, made upon an extensive scale, can lead to any but good results, will not be asserted by any but the few who think that modern observations should only be made to confirm ancient theories. If it is found that a certain condition of brain is an invariable accompaniment of a certain passion; if the condition is more marked when the passion is strong, less marked when it is weak, and unobservable when the passion is wanting; if, moreover, the condition changes with age, waxing and waning as the passion grows or declines,—then the inference becomes almost inevitable, that there is relation of cause and effect; then the external sign by which such internal structure and condition can be known is as much the natural language of the passion as a smile is the natural language of gladness. Now, to say that, because such signs have not yet been satisfactorily ascertained, therefore they never can be ascertained, and that the attempt to ascertain is impious or foolish, is just what it would have been a few years ago to say that, because a nebula never had been resolved, therefore it never could be resolved; that infusoria never had been seen, and therefore never could be seen; and that to turn a telescope to the sky, or the microscope to the water, was impious and foolish.

But however certain it is, first, that the activity and strength of mental manifestations must depend upon the internal structure and condition of the bodily organization; and second, that this structure and condition, like everything material, must have signs and language,—no reference is had to such signs in the following cases.

When it is said that a certain idiot's instinct to fight and destroy is very active, no reference is had to the fulness of his head about the ears; it is meant simply that he strikes, bites, scratches, or smashes things, and thus proclaims, *in another kind of language*, the activity and strength of the propensity. In order to see how many cases there are of coincidence between the craniological development and the existence of the propensity, reference must be had to the Tables.

No. 2. W. C., a lad aged 13 years. BODILY AND MENTAL CONDITION OF PARENTS.—The father is a man of scrofulous temperament, and very puny and feeble both in body and mind. Has been insane at times, especially at religious revivals, at which he prays and exhorts.

The mother is of a similar habit of body and mind, and has always been considered as a simpleton.

They have one other child, a girl aged 20, who is a simpleton.

FUNCTIONS OF ASSIMILATION, DIGESTION, GROWTH, &c. These seem to be pretty active and healthy. He is of the ordinary size, and, though subject to fits when enraged, he has tolerable health.

MUSCULAR VIGOUR, rather below the average.

APPETITE FOR FOOD is insatiable. Unless restrained, he will always so overload his stomach as to bring on fits. He is now limited to a certain ration, which is about double the quantity consumed by other boys of his age. His thirst is also insatiable. He has been known to drink six quarts of water in twenty-four hours.

INSTINCT OF REPRODUCTION does not manifest itself, for he has been carefully watched in this respect.

INSTINCT TO FIGHT AND DESTROY is pretty active. He not only defends himself by striking and scratching, but will rush at things and persons, and push them over. He pulls things to pieces, but does not seem to know how to use his fists to strike, or to handle a stick.

DISPOSITION TO HIDE AND CONCEAL is apparent in the manner in which he disposes of things.

DISPOSITION TO POSSESS AND HOARD is manifested by his claiming his own chair, and his own cup and plate, at table; also by carrying apples and fruit to his room, to put them away.

SELF-ESTEEM is not apparent in any of his actions.

LOVE OF APPROBATION is feebly manifested.

GENERAL ACTIVITY OF SENSES. The five senses are normal, though not acute, except smell.

PERCEPTION OF INDIVIDUAL OBJECTS is feeble. He knows those immediately about him, and the common household things, but he evidently does not know how to recognise persons and things as other children do.

PERCEPTION OF COLOUR unknown.

PERCEPTION OF NUMBER very imperfect; he could not tell the difference between two, three, four and five.

PERCEPTION OF TIME feeble.

PERCEPTION OF MUSICAL SOUNDS null.

FACULTY OF LANGUAGE feebly developed. He knows a few words, but has no power to construct a sentence to express his wants. He hardly knows a hundred words.

CAUSATION he seems to have no sense of whatever. The nearest approach is his habit of stealing hot water and putting it away to cool, in order to gratify his thirst.

DISPOSITION TO IMITATE very feeble: he will pick up chips when he sees other persons doing so, but cannot understand a direction to do so.

BENEVOLENCE utterly wanting: the same with Veneration, Imagination, Conscience, Hope of the Future, &c.

No. 412. Male, aged 24. BODILY AND MENTAL CONDITION OF PROGENITORS.—The mother was a very intemperate prostitute, and not much else is known of her, except that she died of *delirium tremens.*

The father is rather apocryphal.

FUNCTIONS OF HIS GENERAL DEVELOPMENT AND CONDITION OF BODY. Imperfect. Head is very small. The extremities are shortened at the end; that is, the bones of the hands, fingers, and feet, are very short in proportion to the other bones, as if the central formative power had not been vigorous enough to push the growth to the circumference. He is scrofulous, and often covered with sores, scabs, &c.

FUNCTIONS OF ASSIMILATION, DIGESTION, GROWTH, &c., are pretty efficient.

MUSCULAR VIGOUR seems nearly equal to the average. When

sufficient motive is held out, he can do hard work, but the will is wanting because the nervous energy is wanting.

APPETITE FOR FOOD is healthy as to quality of what he eats, but ravenous as to quantity.

INSTINCT FOR REPRODUCTION is fiercely active and ungovernable, and leads him on blindly to excesses of various kinds. The instinct to fight and destroy seems manifested by his instantly resorting to force to destroy whatever opposes his will, —to smash an inanimate object, to kill an animate one, whether it be a fly, a dog, or a child.

No. 358. Aged 22. The mother of this idiot was a very scrofulous and puny person; she was insane during her gestation with him, and died of consumption soon after his birth. She had three children. One was a simpleton, and died young. The other, a sister, is almost idiotic.

The father, a healthy man, married a healthy woman for his second wife, and has five healthy and intelligent children by her.

The head of this idiot is exceedingly small, measuring only 17·5 inches in its greatest circumference, 22 inches being the standard.

The other physical peculiarities need not be referred to here. His language is imperfect, like that of a little child. He understands all simple directions given in sentences short as his own.

There is a useful lesson to be learned from this poor youth's history and treatment. He was formerly very irritable and violent when enraged, breaking and destroying things. For this he was treated in the usual way: force was met by force. He was whipped and punished corporally in various ways, for every offence, by any one about him. As he grew older and stronger, the number of those who could whip him with impunity grew less, till at last the father was obliged to become executioner-general, and in the evening gave him a sound drubbing for the divers and sundry misdemeanours of the day. The father spared not the rod, but healed not the child, who, on the contrary, grew worse and worse. The lessons in punishment were not lost upon him. Whatever object offended him he would beat and punish just as he had been punished. If it were a tool of any kind, he would smash and break it in pieces; if it were a dumb beast, he would beat and abuse it. He smashed rakes, hoes, &c., without number, and one day broke a cow's leg with an axe.

It happened one ovening that a zealous member of the Peace Society was a visitor at the house, and witnessed a scene of contest in which the father barely came off victor. The visitor urged the father to follow a different course with his unfortunate son; to abandon all blows, all direct use of force, and try mild measures. By his advice Johnny was made to understand that, if he should commit a certain offence, he would be mildly and kindly remonstrated with, have nothing but bread and water for supper, and be obliged to lie upon the floor, with only a little straw under him. Very soon he began himself to practise this mode of punishment upon the cattle. If the cow offended him, instead of flying into a passion and beating her, he addressed her gravely, telling her the nature of her offence, and assuring her of the consequences. He would then lead her out, lay some straw upon the ground, bring a little water and a crust of bread, and tell her that was all she could have for supper. One day, being in the field, he hurt his foot with the rake, and instead of getting angry as he was wont to do, and breaking the instrument to pieces, he took it up mildly but firmly, carried it home, got some straw, and laid the offending tool upon it; then he brought some bread and water, and demurely told the offender that it had been very naughty,— that he did not want to hurt it,—but it should have no other supper, and no bed to lie upon.

By such means he has been very much improved, not only in behaviour but in temper. He is growing less violent, and more manageable every day.

This is not at all strange; it is not even different from what happens every day with common children. The poor idiot could not understand much of the spoken words by which *reason* manifests itself, but he could understand the *natural language* of all the passions very well; the angry looks, the harsh voice, the threatening gesture, were felt in the full force of their meaning, and they roused in him the answering feelings of fear, rage, or revenge. These feelings, being called into frequent action, grew more prompt and more fierce by every day's exercise, and would at last have come to be spontaneously and habitually active. But, by withdrawing from before his eyes the natural language of those passions in others, his own were no longer awakened.

As a fierce dog sleeps quietly amid the din of other sounds, but rouses up with defiant growl at the angry bark of another dog, so anger sleeps quietly in our nature, unmoved by anything except *the language of its kind* in another person, which language it understands and answers in a moment. We may make this, and other like passions, sleep so long and so soundly, that they will grow feeble, and even die out ; or we may rouse them up so often that they cannot sleep, even when we will them to do so. The moral of this idiot's history will not be lost upon those whose passions became so restive before they were aware of their nature as to be a source of perpetual trouble in after life, when the moral sense had become awakened to the necessity and the difficulty of self-control.

SIMPLETONS ARE THE HIGHEST CLASS OF IDIOTS, IN WHOM THE HARMONY BETWEEN THE NERVOUS AND MUSCULAR SYSTEM IS NEARLY PERFECT ; WHO CONSEQUENTLY HAVE NORMAL POWERS OF LOCOMOTION AND ANIMAL ACTION ; CONSIDERABLE ACTIVITY OF THE PERCEPTIVE AND AFFECTIVE FACULTIES, AND REASON ENOUGH FOR THEIR SIMPLE INDIVIDUAL GUIDANCE, BUT NOT ENOUGH FOR THEIR SOCIAL RELATIONS.

As the class of fools is much larger than that of idiots, so that of simpletons is much larger than that of fools. Indeed, it is very difficult to estimate their number, or to say what persons shall be included in it, for they can only be measured by a sort of sliding scale, with a standard adapted to different localities and conditions of society. A Russian serf, a Bavarian boor, might enjoy his sinecure office of citizen, and fill his narrow social circle, with a paucity of intellect such as would incapacitate a man for political rights or social relations in Massachusetts. So, among the inhabitants of the *least* intelligent and active village population of Massachusetts, a youth might be thought to be of tolerable capacity, be permitted to go to the polls, and even into society, who would be rated as a simpleton, and treated as such, in the active and bustling crowd of one of our thriving marts, where the weak sink down and disappear, and the strong alone live and thrive. And so it may be with regard to time; a century hence, the standard of intellect and of knowledge may be raised so high as to exclude from the polls, as simpletons, men equal to some of our generation who consider themselves qualified, not only to be citizens, but to hold offices. Who would arrest such progress, provided no qualification but that of knowledge and virtue could ever be required!

The persons put down in this report, as simpletons, are those about whom there could be no doubt, even in this day and generation. They are persons the highest of whom should be considered unable to take any responsibility, to contract matrimony, or to vote. The latter tests, however, should never be applied by interested parties. Some of the simpletons in the list have been wheedled into matrimony, and the bond afterwards cancelled by authority, though nobody can tell how many continue unchallenged. Politicians, too, are sometimes as blind as lovers to the demerits of a head which can command a hand. Several cases have occurred where the taxes were paid for *simpletons*, and they voted—until the opposite party showed that they had a greater number of *fools* whom they could qualify and bring to the polls, and then the poor creatures, who had been used to violate the purity of the ballot and to defraud an election, were thrown aside in contempt.

It has been the aim to include in this report none who could be considered by impartial persons as *compos mentis*. They are susceptible of great improvement, and could be made useful and reputable men, but they cannot be taught in common schools, or trained in the common way.

The following cases will serve as specimens:—

No. 58. H. C. F., aged 33. PARENTAGE.—His mother was extremely intemperate for several years before his birth; she continued to be so for years afterwards, and died of *delirium tremens*. Condition of father not known.

FUNCTIONS OF DIGESTION, ASSIMILATION, GROWTH, &c., seem tolerably well performed. His body is pretty well developed, and his health generally good.

MUSCULAR VIGOUR is impaired by a singular affection of his nervous system, which gives to him the *air, gait,* and *appearance* of *a drunken man!* He seems to have inherited from his mother a strong resemblance to her acquired habit of body.

He trips and staggers in his walk, and frequently falters in his other motions. The nervous fluid seems to flow unsteadily from the brain, or to be frequently wanted; hence the motions of his muscles are suddenly checked, his jaw is arrested in the act of chewing, his lips in the act of speaking ; or, if walking, and the stoppage is considerable, he stumbles, perhaps falls down. Sometimes he remains insensible for a minute or two, and is afterwards utterly unconscious of what passed. More often the command of one muscle, or of one side, is lost for an instant, and he is obliged to hitch and wriggle along with the others. Thus the poor creature drags himself about, a living monument of his mother's shame.

APPETITE FOR FOOD is almost insatiable, and he is very gluttonous. It is said that his mother used to give him rum when he was an infant.

INSTINCT OF REPRODUCTION does not manifest itself in an unnatural degree.

INSTINCT TO FIGHT AND DESTROY is not over active. He does not desire to break things, as some idiots do, but he is ready to fight in self-defence.

INSTINCT TO POSSESS AND HOARD displays itself in his readiness to store up food.

DISPOSITION TO HIDE AND CONCEAL shows itself in the cunning with which he compasses his purpose of obtaining things to eat and of shirking work.

SELF-ESTEEM is manifested in various ways.

LOVE OF APPROBATION is the sentiment most acted upon by those who have the charge of him. To secure the praise and flattery of others, he will do anything in his power.

GENERAL ACTIVITY OF THE FIVE SENSES is normal.

PERCEPTION OF COLOUR is about as usual.

PERCEPTION OF THE RELATIONS OF NUMBER is very imperfect. He can count off, by rote, even to a hundred, but can scarcely tell how much two added to three will make.

PERCEPTION OF TIME is feeble. He keeps step pretty well in walking, but is perplexed in estimating the passage of time.

SENSE OF MUSICAL RELATIONS feeble; he never attempts to sing.

FACULTY OF LANGUAGE is imperfectly developed. He knows the names of individual objects and persons, and can use common sentences, but does not use involutions and complicated expressions.

CAUSALITY seems active in proportion to his other faculties. He can build a fire, wash potatoes, and put them to boil for breakfast, and do similar simple household acts.

DISPOSITION TO IMITATION is not so active as in most persons of his class. Provided he attains an object or an end, he does not seem to care whether he proceeds in the same way that others do or not. In some idiots, this disposition is very strongly marked.

BENEVOLENCE (so little manifested by most idiots) seems active in this man. He is very tender-hearted. His pity is easily excited. He gives away readily of whatever he has.

VENERATION is but feebly manifested. He cares little for his parents, or his elders and superiors—of course, nothing for God.

CONSCIENCE is feebly developed, and he cannot be governed by appeals to it. *Hope* reaches not beyond the things of this life: scarcely beyond the things of to-day.

No. 218. A. B., woman, aged 55, not a pauper. PARENTAGE, &c. Her grandmother was insane, and finally became idiotic. Her mother, and all her brothers and sisters are puny and consumptive. Her youngest sister is stunted in growth, and scarcely *compos mentis*.

FUNCTIONS OF ASSIMILATION, GROWTH, &c., are imperfectly performed. She is hump-backed and nervous.

MUSCULAR VIGOUR, below average; she is incapable of bearing much fatigue.

APPETITE FOR FOOD is natural as to quantity, but her taste has become perverted by use of tea, coffee, spices, &c.

INSTINCT OF REPRODUCTION apparently active, though great pains have been taken to prevent its development. Character in this respect good.

INSTINCT TO FIGHT AND DESTROY is manifested in the degree usual with children. She shows passion sometimes, and if injured retorts, and immediately assails the offender.

DISPOSITION TO POSSESS AND HOARD is not shown in its usual activity; for, though she is desirous of possessing and owning things, she cares not to retain them long.

DISPOSITION TO HIDE AND CONCEAL shows itself not only in

regard to material objects of possession, but sometimes in hypocritical conduct. She will put on certain airs in order to conceal some purpose which she may have.

SELF-ESTEEM is very strongly manifested by its usual natural language. If her simple understanding could be convinced twenty times in a day that she is sadly deficient in every thing of which people are usually vain, it would make no difference; self-esteem springs up again as elastic as ever, and makes her regard herself with great complacency.

LOVE OF APPROBATION is one of the most prominent traits in her character. To gain the attention and praise of others, she will do things that would otherwise be very disagreeable to her.

TENDENCY TO IMITATION is very strong indeed. She does things as she has seen others do them; imitates their actions; and nothing but their example wins her from continual repetition of the same thing in the same manner that she once learned to do it.

THE GENERAL ACTIVITY OF THE SENSES is normal.

PERCEPTION OF INDIVIDUAL OBJECTS, within a certain range, is good. She recognises most of the individuals of the village, and common things about her; but then her circle is narrow, and beyond it she takes no notice of differences between individual objects.

PERCEPTION OF COLOURS is not vivid, but no striking want of power noticed.

PERCEPTION OF NUMBERS limited. With the assistance of *objects*, she can count a score or two, as the number in a pile of plates, the stitches on a knitting needle; but she cannot count or reckon abstractly without the aid of objects. She can count, for instance, a pile of ten or fifteen cents, but cannot tell how many cents are in two or three half dimes. She cannot make change, therefore, or reckon higher than ten, even with the aid of her fingers.

PERCEPTION OF TIME feeble; she can tell the hour by the clock, but without idea of measuring the lapse of time by it.

PERCEPTION OF MUSICAL SOUNDS is apparent in her. She sometimes hums a tune; but no fondness for music has been engrafted upon this capacity, which might have been done.

FACULTY OF LANGUAGE is not well developed ; and her range of words is limited, though she can make simple sentences very well.

PERCEPTION OF CAUSATION is very feeble.

BENEVOLENCE AND CONSCIENCE are feebly manifested.

HOPE is very feeble; the horizon of her future is bounded by to-morrow.

The cases, thus very imperfectly sketched, will serve to give an idea of the different classes of idiotic persons, and of the mode in which the inquiry into their condition was pursued. But they are strongly marked cases each of its kind, and it must not be supposed that all idiotic persons can readily be ranged in one or other of these classes. The highest of the lower class of Idiots can hardly be distinguished from the Fool ; the least stupid of Fools can hardly be distinguished from the Simpleton; and the highest among Simpletons stand very near the level of hundreds who pass in society for feeble-minded persons, but still for responsible free agents. These latter, indeed, are looked down upon by the crowd, but then the crowd is looked down upon by tall men, and these in their turn are looked down upon by the few intellectual giants of each generation who stand higher by the whole head and shoulders than the rest.

This view of the gradation of intellect should teach us not only humility, but humanity ; and increase our interest in those who are only more unfortunate than we are, in that their capacity for seeing and understanding the wisdom, power, and love of our common Father, is more limited than ours, in this stage of our being.

It is thought best not to close this Report without alluding to some

CIRCUMSTANCES OR CAUSES WHICH PREDISPOSE PERSONS TO IDIOCY.

This is a difficult subject, requiring more scientific research and acccuracy than this Report can pretend to. Some facts, however, which have been observed, and some thoughts which have suggested themselves, may possibly be of use to others who follow in this field. When certain circumstances are noted as *preceding* idiocy, it is not meant that they certainly caused it; indeed, it is hard to say that any one cause or condition in a parent will produce idiocy in the offspring; nevertheless, a number of causes united may do it. For instance, take the case

No. 89. Wm. B., aged 13, which is one of idiocy of the lowest kind. This boy cannot walk alone, and can hardly creep about. Has no speech, though some of his natural signs can be understood. He cannot feed himself with a spoon, but can cram food into his mouth with his fingers. His head is very small. His intellect is almost null, and of course the affective faculties are not manifested.

In searching for accompanying circumstances which may throw light upon the probable causes, it is found that the father was a very intemperate man. This is not enough, for all intemperate men do not have idiotic children. His wife was related to him by blood, though not within the degree of first cousin; and still less was this a sufficient cause for the idiocy of the son. The wife's family was tainted with idiocy, her aunt having an idiotic child. We find, therefore, both intermarriage and idiotism in the family; but still this was not cause sufficient, because the parents of this boy had seven other children, all of tolerably good parts.

Looking at the mother's condition during gestation, it is found that, at an early period of it, she was several times very much agitated by terror and mental distress; that at a later one, she became ill, and had great difficulty in carrying her child to its full period; and finally that her confinement was very long, protracted, and painful.

May it not be that these circumstances caused idiocy in this case, though they might not do so in ordinary cases, where the intemperance, or the intermarriage, or the tainted blood, or all of them were wanting? May it not be likewise, that *any one* of these circumstances occurring alone,—the intemperance, the intermarriage, the family taint, the fright, the illness, or the long and difficult parturition,—though it would not cause idiocy, nor even any very manifest effect, might, nevertheless, materially *diminish* what would otherwise have been the bodily and mental vigour of the offspring?

With this explanation, and with the understanding that

probability, and not *certainty*, is aimed at, mention will now be made of some of the *immmediate causes* of idiocy; among which by far the most prolific one is

The low Condition of the Physical Organization of one or both Parents.

It is said by physiologists, that among certain classes of miserably paid and poorly fed workmen, the physical system degenerates so rapidly, that the children are feeble and puny, and but few live to maturity; that the grandchildren are still more puny; until, in the third or fourth generation, the individuals are no longer able to perpetuate their species, and the ranks must be filled up by fresh subjects from other walks of life, to run the same round of deterioration.

It would seem that startled nature, having given warning, by the degenerated condition of three or four generations, at last refuses to continue a race so monstrous upon the earth.

We see here another of those checks and balances which the exhaustless wisdom of God pre-established in the very nature of man, to prevent his utter degeneration. As the comet, rushing headlong towards the sun, is, by the very velocity which it gains, and which seems hurling it into the burning mass, carried safely beyond; so a race of men, abusing the power of procreation, may rush on in the path of deterioration until, arrived at a certain point, a new principle developes itself, the procreating power is exhausted, and that part of the human family must perish, or regain its power by admixture with a less degenerate race.

It will be seen by the tables, that by far the greater part of the idiots are children of parents, one or both of whom were of scrofulous temperament, and poor flabby organization. It is difficult to describe exactly the marks which characterize this low organization, but the eye of a physiologist detects it at once. Regarding it as a matter relating to the mere animal man, if a farmer had swine, cattle, or horses, as inferior to others of their kind as many of these people are inferior to other men and women, he would pronounce them unfit to breed from. Such persons are indeed unfit to continue the species, for, while they multiply the number, they lessen the aggregate powers.

In saying that such persons are generally scrofulous, the word is used in its popular sense, without any pretension to pathological accuracy. Indeed, it is difficult to give a correct idea of scrofula, because its symptoms are so manifold and so various. The class of persons to whom reference is made may be known by several signs. They do not stand erect and firm; they seem rather to be trying to hold their head and shoulders up by their muscles than to rest firmly and gracefully poised upon the spinal column and lower extremities.

Red and sore eyelids, turgid lips, spongy gums, swellings in the glands, liability to eruptions and diseases of the skin, mark this class of persons. The skin is generally fair; the muscles flabby; the hair is light,—seldom hard, crispy and strong. They are not liable to fevers and violent inflammations, as others are, but when unwell nature relieves herself by sores, ulcers, eruptions, &c.

The peccant humours show themselves upon the surface in various ways; swellings and ulcerations of the glands, blotches, tetters, ring worms, rash, salt rheum, &c.

But it is not the surface alone that is affected; the internal tissues are often vitiated, and show their morbid tendencies by various affections, of which cancer is the worst.

Great pains have been taken to ascertain the physical peculiarities of the blood relatives of most of the idiots whose names are upon the list. In reading over the description of more than four hundred families in which idiots are found, one is struck with the great number of cases in which the affections above named are found. A few cases will give a better idea than any general description can do.

No. 289. F. D., aged $4\frac{1}{2}$ years. This child is a poor, puny, and scrofulous creature. Her head is very small, being only 16 inches in circumference. She is quite idiotic, as might be expected with a head of such dimensions upon a frame so weak and low-toned. She is very feeble in the spine; her right side is torpid, and right arm seems paralyzed. Her family is very thriftless and dirty, and present the spectacle, so rare in this country, of sharing their room with the pigs and poultry.

The father is afflicted with salt rheum and other humours, which seem to affect his whole system, and make him dyspeptic and wretched.

The mother is a feeble creature, whose skin is covered with eruptions. One of her children, sister of F. D., lately died from a virulent cancerous affection.

Nos. 129 and 260. Abner and Palmyra H., a brother and sister, aged 33 and 43, both idiotic. Heads small. Bodies of feeble and flabby fibre. The bones of the extremities seem shortened—that is, out of proportion as to length, compared to the body. They are both afflicted with scrofulous humours and sores.

The man shows some of those remarkable signs, often manifested by idiots, of the instincts which one can suppose men would have if in the undeveloped animal state. When a boy, he had a passion *for burrowing in the earth like a rabbit.* He still, at times, will wander off into the woods, dig a hole as for a cellar, collect wood, and go on for days with this occupation, until discovered and brought home.

The general appearance of these idiots is said to be remarkably *like that of their parents when they were in their long drunken debaucheries.*

Both the parents were of unhealthy habit of body, troubled with scrofulous humours, St Anthony's fire, *rum-sores* (as they are called), and other eruptions. All these natural impurities were made worse by intemperance in drink and depravity of life. By temperance, cleanliness, and careful observance of all the natural laws, they might have corrected the vicious humours of their bodies, lived pleasant lives, and been blessed with children to comfort their old age; but they chose to outrage nature in every way, and she sent them their punishment in the shape of those idiotic children.

No. 279. Cynthia T., a girl of 18 years old, idiotic. She was deformed at birth about the eyes and nose. She still shows the marks of a very scrofulous temperament. The bones of the hands and feet are shortened, and the ends seem as if they had been *gnawed* off. The upper edges of the frontal and parietal bones seem shortened, thus reducing the size of the upper part of the brain, or rather, perhaps, being reduced by its non-development.

Her parents, uncles and aunts, cousins, &c., are afflicted, more or less, with St Anthony's fire, salt rheum, cancerous sores, &c.

Her father, as if his constitution was not corrupt enough, poisoned it still more by liquid fire. He has an *idiotic cousin*, who resembles C. T. in many respects.

In seeking for the causes which lead to this sad deterioration of families, it will be found that the most prominent and prolific is

INTEMPERANCE.

By inspection of the tables, it will be seen that, out of 359 idiots, the condition of whose progenitors was ascertained, 99 were the children of drunkards. But this does not tell the whole story by any means. By drunkard is meant a person who is a notorious and habitual sot. Many persons who are habitually intemperate do not get this name even now; much less would they have done so twenty-five or thirty years ago, and many of the parents of the persons named in the tables have been dead longer than that time. A quarter of a century ago a man might go to his bed every night muddled and sleepy with the effects of alcohol, and still not be called an intemperate man.

By pretty careful inquiry as to the number of idiots of the lowest class whose parents were known to be *temperate* persons, it is found that *not one quarter* can be so considered.

The effect of habitual use of alcohol seems to be to *lymphatize* the whole bodily organization; that is, to diminish the proportion of the *fibrous* part of the body—to make the *lymph* abound in all the tissues. The children of such persons are apt to be of the scrofulous character above described; and *their* children are very apt to be feeble in body and weak in mind. Idiots, fools, and simpletons are common among the progeny of such persons. Thus, directly and indirectly, alcohol is productive of a great proportion of the idiocy which now burdens the commonwealth. If, moreover, one considers how many children are born of intemperate parents, who, without being idiots, are deficient in bodily and mental energy, and are *predisposed by their very organization* to have cravings for alcoholic stimulants, it will be seen what an immense burden the drinkers of one generation throw upon the succeeding. Many a parent, by habitual stimulus applied to his own nervous system, forms and fashions his child in such wise, that he is more certain to be made a drunkard by the ordinary temptations of life, than the child of a temperate man would be, even if living from his youth upward within the temptations of a bar-room.

Probably the habitual use of alcoholic drinks does a great deal to bring families into that low and feeble condition of body alluded to in the preceding section, as a prolific cause of idiocy.

There is another vice, a monster so hideous in mien, so disgusting in feature, altogether so beastly and loathsome, that, in very shame and cowardice, it hides its head by day, and, vampyre-like, sucks the very life-blood from its victims by night; and it may perhaps commit more direct ravages upon the strength and reason of those victims than even intemperance; and that vice is

Self-Abuse.

One would fain be spared the sickening task of dealing with this disgusting subject; but as he who would exterminate the wild beasts that ravage his fields must not fear to enter their dark and noisome dens, and drag them out of their lair; so he who would rid humanity of a pest must not shrink from dragging it from its hiding-places, to perish in the light of day. If men deified him who delivered Lerna from its hydra, and canonized him who rid Ireland of its serpents, what should they do for one who could extirpate this monster vice? What is the ravage of fields, the slaughter of flocks, or even the poison of serpents, compared with that pollution of body and soul, that utter extinction of reason, and that degradation of beings, made in God's image, to a condition which it would be an insult to the animals to call beastly, and which is so often the consequence of excessive indulgence in this vice?

It cannot be that such loathsome wrecks of humanity as men and women reduced to drivelling idiocy by this cause, should be permitted to float upon the tide of life, without some useful purpose; and the only one we can conceive, is that of awful beacons to make others avoid,—as they would eschew moral pollution and death,—the course which leads to such ruin.

This may seem to be extravagant language, but there can be no exaggeration, for there can be no adequate description even, of the horrible condition to which men and women are reduced by this practice. There are among those enumerated in this report some who not long ago were considered young gentlemen and ladies, but who are now moping idiots,—idiots of the lowest kind; lost to all reason, to all moral sense, to all shame,—idiots who have but one thought, one wish, one passion,—and that is, the further indulgence in the habit which has loosed the silver cord even in their early youth, which has already wasted, and, as it were, dissolved, the fibrous part of their bodies, and utterly extinguished their minds.

In such extreme cases there is nothing left to appeal to, absolutely less than there is in the dogs and horses; for they may be acted upon by fear of punishment, but these poor creatures are beyond all fear and hope, and they cumber the earth awhile, living masses of corruption.

If only such lost and helpless wretches existed, it would be a duty to cover them charitably with the veil of concealment, and hide them from the public eye, as things too hideous to be seen: but, alas! they are only the *most* unfortunate members of a large class. They have sunk down into the abyss towards which thousands are tending. The vice which has shorn these poor creatures of the fairest attributes of humanity is acting upon others, in a less degree, indeed, but still most injuriously; enervating the body, weakening the mind, and polluting the soul.

A knowledge of the extent to which this vice prevails would astonish and shock many. It is indeed a pestilence which walketh in darkness, because, while it saps and weakens all the higher qualities of the mind, it so strengthens low cunning and deceit, that the victim goes on in his habit unsuspected, until he is arrested by some one whose practised eye reads his sin in the very means which he takes to conceal it—or until all sense of shame is for ever lost in the night of idiocy, with which his day so early closes.

Many a child who confides every thing else to a loving parent conceals this practice in his innermost heart. The sons or daughters who dutifully, conscientiously, and religiously confess themselves to father, mother, or priest, on every other subject, never allude to this. Nay, they strive to cheat and deceive by false appearances; for, as against this darling sin,—duty, conscience, and religion, are all nothing. They even think to cheat God, or cheat themselves into the belief that He who is of purer eyes than to behold iniquity can still regard their sin with favour.

Many a fond parent looks with wondering anxiety upon the puny frame, the feeble purpose, the fitful humours of a dear child, and, after trying all other remedies to restore him to vigour of body and vigour of mind, goes journeying about from place to place, hoping to leave the offending cause behind, while the victim hugs the disgusting serpent closely to his bosom, and conceals it carefully in his vestment.

The evils which this sinful habit works in a direct and positive manner are not so appreciable, perhaps, as that which it effects in an indirect and negative way. For one victim which it leads down to the depths of idiocy, there are scores and hundreds whom it makes shamefaced, languid, irresolute, and inefficient for any high purpose of life. In this way the evil to individuals and to the community is very great.

It behooves every parent, especially those whose children (of either sex) are obliged to board and sleep with other children, whether in boarding-schools, boarding-houses, or elsewhere, to have a constant and watchful eye over them, with a view to this insidious and pernicious habit. The symptoms of it are easily learned, and, if once seen, should be immediately noticed.

Nothing is more false than the common doctrine of delicacy and reserve in the treatment of this habit. All hints, all indirect advice, all attempts to cure it by creating diversions, will generally do nothing but increase the cunning with which it is concealed. The way is, to throw aside all reserve ; to charge the offence directly home ; to show up its disgusting nature and hideous consequences in glowing colours ; to apply the cautery seething hot, and press it on to the very quick, unsparingly and unceasingly.

Much good has been done, of late years, by the publication of cheap books upon this subject. They should be put into the hands of all youth suspected of the vice. They should be forced to attend to the subject. There should be no squeamishness about it.

There need be no fear of weakening virtue by letting it look upon such hideous deformity as this vice presents. Virtue is not salt or sugar, to be softened by such exposure; but the crystal or diamond that repels all foulness from its surface. Acquaintance with such a vice as this,—such acquaintance, that is, as is gained by having it held up before the eyes in all its ugliness,—can only serve to make it detested and avoided.

Were this the place to show the utter fallacy of the notion that harm is done by talking or writing to the young about this vice, it could probably be done by argument, certainly by the relation of pretty extensive experience. This experience has shown that, in ninety-nine cases in a hundred, the existence of the vice was known to the young, but not known in its true deformity; and that, in the hundredth, the repulsive character in which it was first presented made it certain that no further acquaintance with it would be sought.

There is one mode of treatment, however, often recommended by physicians, which in many cases deserves only denouncement as erroneous or sinful;—that is, causing the victim to contract matrimony. The cure is generally effectual, and the mode in which it is accomplished may, in some cases, be justifiable; but certainly, in many others, the retribution of offended nature is awful, and seems like a whole volume of revelation of God's purpose. In no less than ten cases which are here recorded, the idiocy of the children was manifestly attributable to this sin of the parent. Now if a cause, which would be so carefully concealed, is brought out in these ten cases, in how many more must it have been at work unnoticed and unsuspected! And if these ten *extreme* cases of idiocy have been the visitations upon the children of the sins of the parents, how many times ten cases must there be where the visitation is less severe, but still awful! How much bodily disease and weakness; how much mental obliquity and imbecility; how much of ungovernable lust, are thrown upon the children of this generation by the vices of their fathers and mothers of the foregoing one!

There is one remarkable and valuable fact to be learned respecting this vice, from observation of idiots, and that is, that some of them, though they have no idea of right and wrong, no sense of shame, and no moral restraint, are nevertheless entirely free from it. They could never have been in the practice of it, else they would never have abandoned it.

From this may be inferred, that it is a pest generally engendered by too intimate association of persons of the same sex; that it is handed from one to another like contagion; and that those who are not exposed to the contagion are not likely to contract the dreadful habit of it. Hence we see, that not only propriety and decency, but motives of prudence, require us to train up all children to habits of modesty and reserve. Children, as they approach adolescence, should never be permitted to sleep together. Indeed, the rule should be,—not with a view only to preventing this vice, but in view of many other considerations,—that after the infant has left its mother's arms, and become a child, it should ever after sleep in a bed by itself. The older children grow, and the nearer they approach to youth, the more important does this become. Boys even should be taught to shrink sensitively from any unnecessary exposure of person before each other: they should be trained to habits of delicacy and self-respect; and the capacity which nature has given to all for becoming truly modest and refined should be cultivated to the utmost. Habits of self-respect, delicacy, and refinement, with regard to the person, are powerful adjuncts to moral virtues; they need not be confined to the wealthy and favoured classes; they cost nothing: on the contrary, they are the seeds which may be had without price, but which ripen into fruits of enjoyment that no money can buy.

Intermarriage of Relatives.

In assigning this as one of the remote causes of idiocy, it is not meant that, even in a majority of cases, the offspring of marriage between cousins, or other near relations, will be idiotic. The cases are very numerous where nothing extraordinary is observable in the immediate offspring of such unions. On the other hand, there are so many cases where blindness, deafness, insanity, idiocy, or some peculiar bodily or mental deficiency, is seen in such offspring, of the first *or second* generation, that one is forced to believe they cannot be fortuitous. Indeed, the inference seems to be irresistible, that such intermarriages are violations of the natural law, though not such flagrant ones as always to be followed by *obvious* and severe punishment. If two full cousins, who are both in good health, and free from any marked predisposition to any disease or infirmity, should marry, the probability is, that their immediate offspring will have tolerably good constitutions—though no one can say how *much less* vigorous in body and mind they are than would have been offspring born to either parent from marriage with some one of another healthy family. On the other hand, if a man in whose constitution there lurks a predisposition to any particular disease of body or mind, inherited from his *father's* family, should marry a daughter of his *father's* brother or sister, there would be a strong probability that the disease or infirmity would appear in the offspring; while the probability of such re-appearance would be less if he married a healthy cousin by his *mother's* side, and still less if he married a person free from all unhealthy predispositions, who was not related to him at all.

It is seen by the tables, that, out of 359 cases in which the parentage was ascertained, seventeen were *known* to be the children of parents nearly related by blood. But as many of these cases were adults, it was sometimes impossible to ascertain whether their parents, who are dead, were related or not before marriage. From some collateral evidence we conclude, that at least three more cases should be added to the 17. This would show that more than one-twentieth of the idiots examined are offspring of the marriage of relations. Now, as marriages between near relations are by no means in the ratio of one to twenty, nor are even, perhaps, as one to a thousand to the marriages between persons not related, it follows that the proportion of idiotic progeny is vastly greater in the former than in the latter case—(that is, taking this limited number of 400 for what little it is worth as data for calculation). Then it should be considered that idiocy is only *one* form in which nature manifests that she has been offended by such intermarriages. It is believed by some, that blindness, deafness, imbecility, and other infirmities, are more likely to be the lot of the children of parents related by blood than of others. If so, and it seems likely that it is, then the probability of unhealthy or infirm issue from such marriages becomes fearfully great, and the existence of the law against them is made out as clearly as though it were written on tables of stone.

The statistics of the 17 families, the heads of which, being blood relatives, intermarried, tells a fearful tale.

Most of the parents were intemperate or scrofulous; some were both the one and the other; of course, there were other causes to increase chances of infirm offspring, besides that of the intermarriage. There were born unto them *ninety-five* children, of whom FORTY-FOUR were idiotic, twelve others were scrofulous and puny, one was deaf, and one was a dwarf! In some cases, all the children were either idiotic or very scrofulous and puny. In one family of eight children, five were idiotic.

ATTEMPTS TO PROCURE ABORTION.

It appears that out of the idiotic persons examined, at least *seven* were probably made so by attempts, on the part of their mothers, to procure abortion. We say *at least* seven, because it is natural to suppose that, in most cases, every effort would be made to conceal the crime; in many cases the circumstances, even if generally known at the time, would be forgotten in the course of a few years, so that those who had the charge of an idiot twenty or thirty years of age would hardly go back to causes preceding his birth in giving to a stranger an account of the case.

If, then, with all these inducements for secrecy, and all these liabilities to forgetfulness, we find that seven out of about four hundred idiots were made so by attempts at abortion, the probability is very strong that others, whose history we do not know, were made idiotic by the same dreadful crime. Attempts are sometimes made by young women to conceal their shame by getting rid of their unborn proof of it; but, failing in this, they get married, and the child is idiotic, though all children born afterwards of the same parents are sound and healthy. Several cases of this kind are among those above alluded to. One woman had *seven* sound children, and another had *six*, born in wedlock, though the oldest child of each of them, upon whom abortion was attempted, was idiotic.

This subject is indeed most painful. It is horrible to think that a mother should aim a blow at the life of her unborn babe, and failing of murder, wound and maim his soul, and bring forth a drivelling idiot to be a life-long witness against her crime ; but such is one of the forms in which the fruit of sin reappears to punish the sinner and forewarn all beholders.

There is nothing which nature so carefully guards as the *life* of her creatures. This must be secured, if necessary, at the expense of everything else. This care is manifested from the first moment of conception. The tender being hidden in the innermost and vital centre of its mother, floating in an elastic fluid, and carefully enveloped, fold within fold, by curious membranes, is not only beyond her reach, but almost beyond the reach of accident. She may fall—her bones may be broken —she may be wounded even unto death—and her babe be still safe. She may, it is true, affect its health by her own intemperance in food or drink ; she may affect its passions by indulging her own, but still it lives.

Now, the attempt to destroy what nature so carefully guards is a most dangerous one ; and it can only succeed by using medicines or measures of such violence that the whole system is shaken to its centre, and the life of the mother put in peril in order to kill the babe. The attempts, however violent, may fail ; they do fail, perhaps, oftener than they succeed ; but, alas! the poor innocent who has escaped murder has not escaped injury. It cannot be doubted that many are made idiotic, and more have their faculties impaired, and their bodies injured, by attempts at this unnatural crime.

Sceptical persons may naturally inquire how it is possible for the Commissioners to procure any reliable information concerning matters of this kind, since the parties would not be likely to criminate themselves. It is to be recollected, however, that most of such persons are very ignorant and indiscreet; that some of them do not perceive any guilt in an attempt to destroy evidence of shame; that women are very communicative; and that an inquisitive person, whose object was evidently only to learn all he could about an idiotic child, solely with a view to the good of that child, would obtain evidence not easily obtained from others.

Matters like these soon become known among the friends

and neighbours of the parties, if they are of the ignorant class, and are spoken about without much reserve.

It may be said about this, as about supposed causes of idiocy referred to above, that great care has been taken to obtain evidence; that much has been suppressed which was deemed doubtful; and that the rest is given with such explanations of its source, that each one may place upon it as much reliance as he think it deserves.

We have thus alluded to some of the most obvious and fertile causes (either remote or proximate) of the existence of such a great number of idiots as are found in this, and all other countries called civilized. It would swell this Report to volumes, to examine these causes pathologically and minutely. Scientific research has not been our object, but we have sought diligently for every item and scrap of knowledge upon the subject of idiocy which could be of practical use to the legislature. In so doing we have been obliged in some cases to drag, as with a net, the lower depths of society, seeking for the pearls of truth. With those pearls there may be much worthless trash, but this will all perish, while the gems will remain indestructible; and, if they are of value enough to redeem only one human being from the brutishness of idiocy, our labours will not be in vain.

For the Commission,

S. G. HOWE.

GENERAL EXPLANATION OF THE TABLES.

The Commissioners, after visiting and inspecting personally many idiots, found that it was very important that a minute examination should be made of a very large number of those unfortunate persons, and full information obtained concerning their history, and the habits and bodily condition of their immediate progenitors, in order that some general inferences might be drawn concerning the causes of their calamity. It was impossible for any one of the Commissioners to devote himself solely to a work requiring so much time. Mr Enos Stevens, a young gentleman of good character, was therefore engaged for this purpose. He had been employed in making measurements of the human body, with a view to certain physiological studies, and was thus partly qualified for the task. A series of questions was drawn up for him. He was occupied the whole of the last summer (1847) in collecting information, visiting all the idiots in a large number of towns, and spending from an hour to half a day in examining each one of them, and making thorough inquiries of their relatives concerning their history. The great mass of his *field notes* have been as carefully examined, sifted, and digested by the Commissioners, as the pressure of other occupations would allow; and the result will be found in the following tabular summary. It has no pretensions to science in arrangement, or perfect accuracy in the details. Others might have elicited more truth, and eliminated more errors. It is submitted with a consciousness of its imperfections, but a confidence in its general correctness.

EXPLANATION OF TABLE No. 1.

The object of this table is to furnish data for a comparison between idiots and ordinary persons, in certain respects.

Some of the columns furnish positive information which can be relied upon, as age, dimensions, &c. Others furnish only the means of approximating to the truth. In judging of the temperament, for instance, one observer will describe a person as being more nervous than fibrous, while another observer might reverse the order.

The mode adopted for showing the comparison, though it may seem preposterous with respect to *certain mental qualities*, is, on the whole, the best that could be thought of by the Commissioners. For instance,—it may seem idle to talk about the activity of the moral sentiments in one man being as 5, while in another man it is 6, or 4, or 10. But it is not seen how any better mode could be found, without printing all the particulars of each case, which would make a voluminous work. The mode adopted was this: Assuming there is a moral sense, resulting from the tolerably harmonious action of the various mental faculties, and that the degree of its activity in ordinary persons is represented by 10, the idiot is examined, and, if he has no sense of property, no idea of right, no benevolence, no affection or regard for anybody, he is marked, 0. If he has some faint idea of property, he is marked 1; if he has affections, 2; if he manifests the rudiments of veneration, by respect for others, 4, or 5, &c. Some are marked higher than ordinary individuals, and this may seem still more idle, since a great activity of the moral sense implies intelligence of uncommon order; nevertheless, as, in these persons, the disposition to venerate and obey elders or superiors, to respect property, to feel pity, and show affection, are more apparent than in ordinary persons of *their age and condition of life*, they are marked higher in the moral sense.

It matters not whether the psychological estimate here made of moral sense be correct or not, so that the reader knows what mental qualities were referred to in making up the table. It will be seen that, to obtain information which would enable one even to approximate to a correct estimate of character, each idiot must be examined personally and closely, and a great variety of questions put to those who have the care of him; and this was done. Whenever the measurements of the cranium are given, they may be depended upon as accurate, having been carefully taken with a cephalometer.

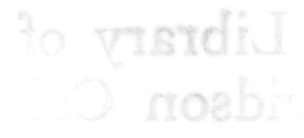

It is pretty well ascertained that the activity of certain mental faculties or moral sentiments has some relation to the actual size of different parts of the cranium;—for instance, that where the lateral region of the cranium is full or protuberant, the faculties of self-preservation, forethought as to food and raiment, cunning, &c., will be manifested in greater activity than in those cases where that region is flat, other things being equal. Now, when these measurements were taken in idiots, care was also taken to ascertain the peculiarities of the character; and the results of the two observations are placed side by side, for the gratification of the curious.

AGE.—The average age of congenital idiots, as appears by this column, is 29 years. This, however, is not the average longevity of idiots, because no reference is had to the number that were born, but only the number and ages of those *now living*. According to the best estimate that can be made by the Commissioners, the average duration of life of congenital idiots is not more than 12 years. There are a great number brought into the world so deformed, that it is apparent they must be idiotic, and so feeble that they do not live through infancy.

Idiots of the lowest class perish in great numbers in infancy and childhood; fools last longer, and simpletons attain to nearly the ordinary longevity. Perhaps it is safe to say, that the average longevity of the lowest class of idiots is not more than 6 years.

2d Column, CONGENITAL, OR NOT.—When the person appeared, in infancy or early childhood, to be idiotic, he is considered to have been born so.

3d Column, HEIGHT.—It has not been possible to procure the height of a sufficient number of persons of Massachusetts to establish a standard of comparison.

TEMPERAMENTS.—There is not much reliable information to be gathered, perhaps, from these four columns. The object was, however, to show, in each case, the kind of original structure of body or the acquired habits. For instance, if a certain person has the brain and nervous system originally large and well developed; or if, by the quickness of his motions, his general sensibility, the acuteness of his senses, and other appearances, he gives signs of that system being in great activity, while his arterial, muscular, and glandular systems are less developed, he is marked nervous, first; sanguine, second, &c. If, on the contrary, his brain and nervous system are comparatively small, or if he is sluggish and insensible, while the glandular system is well developed, and he eats, and sleeps, and lounges about, and grows fat; he is marked lymphatic first, and nervous last.

Fibrous temperament is used as a better term than bilious. It expresses the preponderance of the *fibre* of the body; that which gives strength and endurance, or toughness. A man of fibrous temperament is one whose osseous system is well developed, all the prominences on the bones being strongly marked, making the body angular, and the features sharp and strong; whose muscles have no fat, but seem like bundles of wires; whose hair is hard, and wiry, and black, and who is capable of great endurance.

Now, it is very rare to find a person who is decidedly and strongly of one temperament. The temperaments are generally united, but one preponderates over the others, and the order of this preponderance among idiotic persons is attempted to be shown in these tables.

TACTILE SENSIBILITY.—By this is meant the activity of the sense of feeling residing upon the surface of the body. There is great difference in this respect, and this does not arise from the fact that the nervous system generally is well developed or not.

For instance; No. 210 is a girl 19 years old. The surface of her body is comparatively insensible; flies and insects would hardly be felt; the prick of a pin, or the extraction of a hair, would not cause half the sensation shown by ordinary persons. She is marked 4. But she is quite animated by the sound of music, and will even leave off eating to listen to it; therefore, in the column indicating sensibility to musical sounds, she is marked 13. The average of tactile sensibility in this class of persons, compared with ordinary persons, is as $8\frac{1}{2}$ to 10.

COMMAND OF MUSCULAR CONTRACTILITY.—This indicates the degree of command or *direction* over the muscles which a person possesses. The difference among men in this respect is immense, and is not all dependent upon the *dynamic condition or strength of body*, indicated in the next column. Many of what are called the *involuntary* muscles, as some of the sphincters, are nevertheless considerably under the command of the will in ordinary circumstances, and the command is sometimes lost, as by sudden and great fright, especially in young persons. In idiots, these sphincters are much less under the command of the will. Children are sometimes severely punished because they 'have not naturally so much muscular contractility as others, and the sphincters relax when they sleep.

Take case No. 218. This woman is marked 11 in the column showing command of muscular contractility; she is unusually agile, and can command the muscles of her body and hands, and work very expertly at anything she can understand; but, under column for dynamic condition of body, she is marked only 7, because she is below the average of strength. Some jugglers attain to uncommon command of muscular contractility, without much muscular power.

DYNAMIC CONDITION OF BODY, or general vigour of health, as manifested in the ability to put forth muscular strength. The average is as 8 to 10; this is probably too high.

SENSIBILITY TO MUSICAL SOUNDS.—The meaning of this is obvious. There is very great difference in this respect among idiots; and the degree of sensibility to musical sounds is by no means commensurate with intellectual ability. Some very stupid idiots can sing correctly, and detect a false note instantly. The average is as 6 to 10.

SKILL IN THE USE OF LANGUAGE.—As a general rule, this is the surest test of the degree of intelligence. It is not the amount of *talking*, but the number and variety of words at their command, that must be considered. Some who are garrulous to the last degree, chattering all the time, and repeating over and over all day long the few words and phrases they know, are, nevertheless, marked very low in this column; while others, who talk much less, are marked higher, because they have knowledge of a much greater number of words.

CAPACITY FOR FIXING SIGHT UPON VISIBLE OBJECTS.—The markings in this column are probably too high. The faculty depends somewhat upon degree of command of muscular contractility. Some who have visual organs which seem perfect, can with difficulty fix the sight upon a small object, as a hair. Those who are marked 0 are blind.

ABILITY TO COUNT.—There is very great difference in this respect; but the degree of ability is not at all indicative of the degree of intelligence. Those marked 0 cannot count at all; if they have three apples, and you abstract one slily, they do not perceive the loss. Some will miss one apple out of a heap of three or four, but will not miss one if taken from a heap of five or six. Such cases are marked 2 or 3; while, if they can count ten, they would be marked 4. Sometimes they have great quickness at simple reckoning. No. 225 has little use of language; he is marked but 4 in that column; his intellect is very limited; he is, to all intents, an idiot; yet he has an astonishing power of reckoning. Tell him your age, and he will, in a very short time, give you the number of minutes. He is marked 18; he should, perhaps, have been marked higher. The average is as 3 to 10.

CONSUMPTION OF FOOD.—The column expresses, as nearly as could be, the amount of food consumed in comparison with other persons. None are marked higher than 20, though some are perfectly insatiable, and, if they can get at food, though it be swill, they gorge themselves, vomit, and then gorge again. Even in cases where they have a given allowance, they will contrive to beg or steal more. It is difficult to know where to rank such cases, or how to express the degree of their voracity by any number. The average by the table is as 15 to 10.

MANIFESTATION OF AMATIVE FEELINGS.—In this column it is attempted to show the degree of activity of the sexual passion. This is measured by the sexual desire, which is manifested in various ways, either natural or diseased. In some cases it amounts to a perfect mania. The physical powers yield, break down, and seem exhausted, but the horrid propensity continues unabated. Average marked as $16\frac{1}{2}$ to 10.

The next columns in order are those giving the actual measurements of different parts of the body, and especially of the cranium and its different parts. They were taken with great care, and are believed to be exact.

DEGREE OF ABILITY TO SUPPORT THEMSELVES.—This column, of course, gives only an approximate estimate, because an idiot, under the care of discreet and industrious persons, would be made to do much towards his own support, whereas, under the care, or rather under the neglect, of ignorant and idle parents, he would be a drone.

PARENTS IN A NORMAL CONDITION OF HEALTH, OR NOT.—This column is intended to show the number of cases in which *both* parents of the idiot were usually in the enjoyment of vigorous health before his birth.

Where both parents were sound and healthy, so as to be able to pursue their avocations steadily and uninterruptedly, to eat heartily, and sleep soundly, they are considered as healthy. If either of them was puny, obliged frequently to give up labour on account of indisposition; if they were dyspeptic, or subject to scrofulous humours and sores; or if they had been insane within two or three years before the birth of the child, they are considered not to have been in a normal state of health.

PARENTS DRUNKARDS, OR NOT.—This column cannot be taken as a test of the number of idiots whose parents were *intemperate* before their birth. It shows only how many carried their intemperance to such an extent that they were set down, by universal consent, as drunkards. Some of these are the parents of persons forty or fifty years old. Of course, they lived in a time when a man must have been continually besotted with strong drinks before he would be called a drunkard.

NUMBER OF CASES OF IDIOCY OR INSANITY KNOWN AMONG NEAR RELATIVES.—This means to express the number of cases in which there was, among the immediate kindred of the idiot, one or more idiotic or insane persons; that is, among those who stood to him in the relation of grand-parent, parent, child, uncle, aunt, brother, sister, nephew, niece, or first cousin. Of course, these are sometimes repeated; as when there are two idiots who are brothers.

SCROFULOUS, OR NOT.—This is a very vague and unsatisfactory term; and, in this case, it is employed in its most comprehensive sense. If persons are much subject to frequent eruptions, boils, ulcers, deep-seated humours, colds and coughs; if the flesh, when wounded, will not heal readily; if indisposition seldom or never takes the form of fever, but appears in chronic affections of different organs, they are supposed to be scrofulous. They *usually* have *fair* skin ; they have grains or swellings among the glands, red and spongy gums, and rather flabby flesh. Sometimes they may be apparently in good health, and be marked as normal in the dynamic condition of the body, being, at the time of observation, pretty vigorous, while these symptoms of scrofulous habit of body are still apparent. It is common for persons having the care of idiots to say of them that they are going to be sick, because all their eruptions and humours have dried up; or to say they will surely be well for some months, because boils and humours are making their appearance.

GIVEN TO MASTURBATION, OR NOT.—This means that the person is *known* to be habitually in the practice of this vice.

TEACHABLE, OR NOT.—That is, whether they appear to have capacity enough to be improved in their habits, and made to do simple work.

In the column for General Remarks, some peculiar or striking circumstance is given relating to the case ; generally, but not always, such as are supposed to have had influence in causing the idiocy. Sometimes it is stated very positively by the relatives, or even physicians, that the idiocy was occasioned by causes that alone are altogether inadequate, such as severe salivation in infancy: where no other remarkable circumstance is known, this one is put down.

TABLE No. I.

SHOWING

THE PHYSICAL AND MENTAL CONDITION

OF

IDIOTIC PERSONS

IN

MASSACHUSETTS.*

---

* [It has been thought sufficient to reprint merely a specimen of this Table, as a guide to future observers. The entire Table, as printed by the Commissioners, exhibits the condition of 574 idiots, the facts respecting whom are summed up in the other Tables, which are given here without abridgment.]

TABLE NO. I.

Numbers for reference to names in the MSS.	Age.	Congenital Idiocy, or not.	Height, in feet and inches.	Comparisons with ordinary persons, Ten being the standard, lower numbers making inferiority, and higher numbers superiority.											
				Temperaments expressed in the order of their preponderance. n. for nervous. f. „ fibrous. s. „ sanguine. l. „ lymphatic.				Tactile Sensibility.	Command of Muscular Contractility.	Dynamic Condition of Body.	Sensibility to Musical Sounds.	Skill in the use of Language.	Capacity for fixing Sight upon visible objects.	Ability to Count.	Consumption of Food.	Manifestation of Amative Feelings.
1	60	Yes	5 ft. 2½ in.	n.	f.	s.	l.	9	8	6	5	3	9	1	16	5
2	13	Yes	4 ft. 8½ in.	s.	l.	n.	f.	10	6	3	...	5	8	1	20	1
3	28	Yes	5 ft.	s.	l.	f.	n.	9	9	11	4	5	9	3	16	3
4	29	Yes	5 ft. 4½ in.	s.	f.	l.	n.	8	9	12	8	2	10	1	14	19
5	25	Yes	5 ft. 4 in.	s.	n.	f.	l.	8	8	10	...	4	10	2	10	9
6	25	Yes	5 ft. 5 in.	f.	s.	n.	l.	9	10	12	...	5	10	3	10	9
7	37	Yes	5 ft. 3½ in.	l.	f.	n.	s.	8	6	5	...	6	10	2	10	8
8	22	Yes	5 ft. 9½ in.	s.	f.	l.	n.	9	10	11	...	8	10	3	11	10
9	60	Yes	5 ft. 10 in.	s.	n.	l.	f.	9	10	9	...	8	10	3	10	8
10	58	Yes	5 ft. 6 in.	f.	s.	l.	f.	7	8	6	...	2	9	2	8	...
11	15	Yes	5 ft. 1 in.	f.	l.	n.	s.	10	9	9	11	8	10	6	10	9
12	60	Yes	5 ft. 6 in.	f.	n.	s.	l.	8	2	3	2	2	8	3	9	10
13	15	Yes	5 ft.	n.	l.	s.	l.	10	8	8	7	7	9	5	10	10
14	23	Yes	5 ft. 5 in.	n.	f.	s.	l.	12	7	8	...	6	6	3	10	10
15	21	Yes	4 ft. 11 in.	l.	s.	f.	n.	6	5	3	...	5	9	1	10	9
16	47	Not	5 ft. 6 in.	f.	n.	s.	l.	8	9	9	6	9	10	4	10	9
17	65	Not	5 ft. 3½ in.	n.	f.	s.	l.	8	10	10	...	8	10	6	10	6
18	13	Yes	4 ft. 7 in.	n.	f.	l.	s.	12	6	6	...	8	8	4	9	8
19	10	Yes	4 ft.	l.	s.	f.	n.	7	8	11	...	3	9	1	20	3
20	12	Yes	4 ft. 4 in.	n.	f.	s.	l.	9	2	1	...	2	8	1	12	3
21	17	Yes	5 ft. 8 in.	f.	s.	l.	n.	7	9	10	6	8	10	5	12	14
22	28	Not	5 ft. 6 in.	l.	s.	n.	f.	9	10	9	10	8	8	8	16	20
23	30	Yes	5 ft. 1 in.	f.	n.	s.	l.	8	4	8	8	7	8	4	14	19
24	12	Yes	4 ft. 1 in.	n.	s.	f.	l.	10	10	9	...	7	10	3	16	2
25	23	Yes	5 ft. 4 in.	n.	f.	s.	l.	10	9	12	8	7	10	2	12	10
26	15	Yes	5 ft.	f.	s.	n.	l.	8	9	10	3	2	9	1	18	...
27	59	Yes	5 ft. 4 in.	f.	s.	n.	l.	7	9	9	12	6	10	4	20	18
28	19	Yes	5 ft. 4 in.	n.	f.	s.	l.	9	8	9	7	6	9	2	14	10
29	45	Yes	5 ft. 1 in.	n.	f.	s.	l.	8	3	6	...	7	8	3	15	...
30	19	Yes	5 ft. 3 in.	f.	l.	s.	n.	9	10	8	6	8	10	6	12	...
31	28	Yes	5 ft. 8 in.	n.	s.	f.	l.	9	10	8	...	8	10	4	13	...
32	8	Yes		...	...	...	...	...	...	...	...	...	...	...	...	...
33	3	Yes	...	l.	f.	s.	n.	3	2	1	0	1	3	0	10	...
34	19	Yes	...	...	...	...	...	...	3	...	...	...	...	2	12	...
35	8	Yes	3 ft. 2 in.	n.	f.	s.	l.	10	14	18	...	0	10	1	20	...
36	25	Not	5 ft. 9 in.	f.	l.	s.	n.	2	7	9	...	2	8	1	18	20
37	41	Yes	5 ft. 3 in.	f.	n.	s.	l.	9	10	12	...	7	10	2	18	16
38	36	Not	...	...	...	...	...	...	...	...	...	...	...	4	10	...
39	25	Yes	5 ft. 3 in.	f.	l.	n.	s.	8	6	3	8	5	10	3	10	...
40	52	Not	5 ft. 8 in.	n.	s.	f.	l.	9	8	9	...	4	10	3	10	20
41	49	Yes	...	f.	s.	n.	l.	7	8	9	...	3	10	1	20	20
42	60	Yes	5 ft. 7 in.	l.	s.	n.	f.	6	4	4	...	5	9	3	14	...
43	39	Yes	5 ft. 1 in.	n.	f.	s.	n.	7	8	9	...	2	9	1	10	10
44	44	Yes	5 ft. 5 in.	f.	n.	l.	s.	10	10	9	0	6	0	3	10	...
45	55	Not	5 ft. 10 in.	f.	l.	s.	n.	8	9	6	...	8	10	7	10	12

TABLE NO. I.

Numbers for reference to names in the MSS.	Actual size, by Measurement, in inches and tenths.								Development of various parts of the cranium, and activity of various mental faculties, as compared with that of 1000 ordinary persons of the same age and sex; 10 being the standard among ordinary persons.									
	Depth of Chest.	Width of Chest.	Greatest Circumference of Cranium.	Greatest Diameter of Cranium.	Diameter from the root of the Nose to the Occipital Spine.	Transverse Diameter over the Ears.	Arc of Cranium from Root of Nose to Occipital Spine.	Arc from Ear to Ear.	Size of the Lower Frontal Region.	Skill in the use of the Perceptive Faculties.	Size of the Upper Frontal Region.	Skill in the use of the Reflective Faculties.	Size of the Lateral Region.	Activity of the Faculties of Self-Preservation.	Size of the Posterior Region.	Activity of the Social Attachments.	Size of the Coronal Region.	Activity of the Moral Sentiments.	Size of the Cerebellum.	Activity of the Animal Nature.	Degree of ability to support themselves.
1	8	11·2	22·5	7·8	7·7	5·8	14	11·2	15	3	17	1	12	4	7	7	10	12	6	9	4
2	7	8·5	...	7·3	7·3	5·4	...	...	12	3	11	2	15	8	10	4	10	2	11	7	2
3	8	10·2	...	7	...	5·5	12·8	13·5	4	4	5	3	6	7	4	6	3	11	6	10	4
4	9	11	22	7·5	7·5	5·8	...	...	9	3	8	1	10	4	9	2	8	1	10	14	3
5	9	9·5	22	7·7	7·7	5·3	13·5	14·2	10	3	9	2	6	3	9	6	8	9	7	11	3
6	8·5	9·5	22	7·9	7·9	5·5	13·3	14·1	10	4	9	3	8	4	11	7	8	9	9	10	4
7	8·2	10	...	6·8	6·8	5·3	13·5	14	8	4	11	2	8	6	1	10	8	9	1	8	4
8	8·5	10	23	7·8	7·8	5·7	14·5	15·5	13	5	16	5	10	6	10	10	17	9	8	11	5
9	8·5	10·5	...	8·3	8·3	5·8	...	...	13	8	14	4	12	2	10	8	15	9	12	9	5
10	...	...	...	7·5	7·5	5·4	...	...	8	3	11	4	8	8	11	2	12	10	8	6	4
11	7	8·5	...	7	7	5·1	...	...	6	4	3	3	2	1	1	6	1	3	1	9	4
12	8	9	...	7·4	7·4	5·4	...	...	8	3	11	4	9	6	6	4	9	6	5	7	3
13	7·5	7·8	...	8	7·9	5·7	...	...	11	6	12	5	11	3	14	10	13	10	8	9	5
14	7·5	10	...	7·7	7·7	5·6	...	...	11	6	7	5	9	3	8	4	8	7	6	9	4
15	7	9·5	...	7·2	7·2	5·4	...	...	10	2	11	3	7	5	3	8	7	8	7	7	2
16	8·2	10·2	...	8·2	8·1	5·6	...	...	11	8	13	8	11	2	15	4	13	10	14	9	5
17	8	10	...	8	7·9	5·2	...	...	8	8	11	7	6	1	14	6	9	9	8	8	6
18	5·8	9	...	8	7·8	5·2	...	...	13	6	12	4	6	2	7	10	7	10	1	7	5
19	5·8	7·7	...	7·4	7·4	5·3	...	...	9	2	11	1	10	4	12	8	11	3	9	11	2
20	7	7·7	...	...	6·7	5·6	...	...	10	1	9	1	12	2	3	4	13	3	6	5	1
21	8·5	10·5	...	...	...	...	...	...	...	3	...	3	...	7	...	6	...	10	...	12	4
22	...	...	...	...	...	...	...	...	...	8	...	8	...	2	...	8	...	4	...	14	5
23	6·5	10	...	7·1	7·1	5·4	...	...	8	6	6	5	3	3	1	8	4	7	1	14	4
24	6·5	8·5	...	7·7	7·5	5	...	...	10	6	11	4	5	3	7	8	12	9	1	9	4
25	7·5	8·8	...	7·7	7·7	5·6	...	...	10	8	9	3	7	4	10	6	9	10	5	11	4
26	6·8	8·6	...	7·4	7·4	5·4	...	...	8	3	9	1	7	1	7	2	11	6	6	14	3
27	8·9	10·2	...	7·8	7·7	5·7	...	...	15	8	15	5	10	2	9	4	12	5	7	16	5
28	7·5	9·5	...	7·8	7·8	5·5	...	...	10	4	11	4	9	4	11	7	12	10	8	11	4
29	7·1	9·7	...	7·1	7·1	5	...	...	6	3	1	2	1	2	1	3	1	4	2	11	3
30	7·9	9·1	20	6·8	6·8	5·2	12·2	13	5	5	3	6	8	7	1	7	2	10	5
31	8·2	10	...	7·5	7·5	5·4	...	...	11	8	5	6	5	3	6	4	1	6	5	10	5
32	...	...	...	...	...	...	...	...	...	4	...	3	...	3	...	5	...	6	...	3	4
33	...	...	...	...	...	...	...	...	...	1	...	0	...	0	...	0	...	0	...	1	0
34	...	...	...	...	...	...	...	...	...	3	...	2	...	2	...	3	...	2	...	12	3
35	...	...	...	5·3	5·3	4·7	...	...	...	4	...	1	...	5	...	0	...	0	...	19	2
36	9	10·2	...	8·2	8·2	6	...	...	11	2	9	1	12	1	14	1	14	1	9	16	4
37	7·6	10	...	7·1	7	5·5	...	...	4	4	5	5	6	3	4	2	6	4	2	16	4
38	...	...	...	...	...	...	...	...	...	4	...	5	...	4	...	5	...	6	...	...	5
39	6	8·3	...	7·3	7·3	5·2	...	...	4	4	8	6	7	2	7	9	4	8	2	6	5
40	8·2	10·5	...	7·9	7·9	6·1	...	...	12	5	11	9	13	3	9	8	14	6	9	11	5
41	9	11	...	7·7	7·7	5·6	...	...	11	3	10	2	8	2	7	3	7	1	8	16	3
42	8·7	10	...	8	7·9	6·2	...	...	15	6	17	5	17	4	12	6	17	5	5	9	4
43	8·3	9·2	...	7·7	7·6	5·2	...	...	7	2	8	4	6	3	11	7	8	6	9	10	3
44	8·9	9·6	...	6·8	6·8	4·6	...	...	1	4	6	6	4	5	6	4	6	1	9	4
45	9	10·6	...	8·2	8·1	6	...	...	15	7	16	9	13	5	13	4	16	4	9	9	6

D

TABLE NO. I.

Numbers for reference to names in the MSS.	Parents in normal condition of health, or not.	Parents Drunkards, or not.	Number of cases of Idiocy or Insanity known among near relatives.	Scrofulous, or not.	Given to Masturbation, or not.	Teachable, or not.	REMARKS.
1	...	...	...	Yes	Not	Yes	Always healthy.
2	Not	Not	3	Yes	Not	Yes	Subject to fits; mother insane during gestation.
3	Not	...	...	Yes	Not	Yes	Head small, swinish; skin pachydermatous.
4	Not	Yes	...	Yes	Yes	Yes	Head and voice resemble swine; skin pachydermatous.
5	Not	Not	3	Yes	...	Yes	
6	Not	Not	3	Yes	...	Yes	
7	Not	...	2	Yes	...	Not	
8	Not	Yes	3	Yes	Yes	Yes	
9	Not	Not	1	Not	Not	Yes	
10	...	...	...	Yes	...	Not	
11	Not	...	1	Yes	Not	Yes	
12	Not	...	None	Yes	Not	Not	Subject to fits in youth.
13	Yes	Yes	None	Not	Not	Yes	Subject to fits from 1 to 5 years old.
14	Not	...	...	Yes	Not	Yes	Subject to fits in infancy and youth.
15	Not	Not	3 or 4	Yes	Not	Yes	Parents related by blood.
16	...	...	None	Not	Not	Yes	Intemperate in youth.
17	...	...	...	Not	Not	Yes	Supposed cause, disappointment in love and business
18	Not	Not	None	Yes	Not	Yes	[at 30 years of age.
19	Not	Yes	...	Yes	Not	Not	
20	Not	...	None	Yes	Not	Yes	Supposed to have suffered from laudanum in infancy.
21	Not	Not	3	Yes	Yes	Yes	
22	Yes	Not	...	Yes	Yes	Yes	Supposed cause, masturbation.
23	Not	Yes	2	Yes	Yes	Yes	
24	Not	Yes	4	Yes	...	Yes	Subject to fits.
25	Not	...	...	Yes	Not	Yes	Puny and sickly in infancy.
26	Not	...	2	Yes	Yes	Yes	Parents monomaniacs.
27	Not	Yes	1	Yes	Yes	Yes	
28	Not	...	1	Yes	Not	Yes	
29	Not	Not	None	Yes	...	Yes	Very small head.
30	Not	Yes	1	Yes	...	Yes	Parents intemperate, and brother idiotic.
31	Not	...	None	Yes	Yes	Yes	Very puny in youth.
32	Not	Not	None	Yes	...	Yes	Supposed to have suffered from drugs in infancy.
33	Not	Yes	None	Yes	Not	d'bt'l	
34	Not	...	...	Yes	...	Yes	Subject to fits and paralysis.
35	Not	Yes	None	Yes	...	Yes	
36	...	...	None	Yes	Yes	Yes	Idiotic at 18, from masturbation.
37	Not	Yes	1	Yes	Yes	Yes	Very small head.
38	...	...	...	Yes	...	Yes	Supposed cause, fits at 8 years old.
39	Not	...	None	Yes	...	Yes	Mother sickly during gestation.
40	...	Not	...	Yes	Yes	Yes	Idiotic from 5 years old.
41	Not	...	...	Yes	Yes	Yes	Masturbation and gluttony from childhood.
42	...	...	...	Yes	Yes	Yes	General torpor, or paralysis.
43	...	...	...	Yes	Not	Yes	
44	...	...	...	Yes	Not	Yes	Very small head. [intemperance.
45	...	...	...	Yes	Yes	Yes	Supposed cause, venereal excesses and diseases, and

TABLE NO. I.   51

Numbers for reference to names in the MSS.	Age.	Congenital Idiocy, or not.	Height, in feet and inches.	Comparisons with ordinary persons, Ten being the standard, lower numbers marking inferiority, and higher numbers superiority.					Tactile Sensibility.	Command of Muscular Contractility.	Dynamic Condition of Body.	Sensibility to Musical Sounds.	Skill in the use of Language.	Capacity for fixing Sight upon visible objects.	Ability to Count.	Consumption of Food.	Manifestation of Amative Feelings.
				Temperaments expressed in the order of their preponderance.													
				n. for nervous. f. „ fibrous. s. „ sanguine. l. „ lymphatic.													
46	47	Yes	5 ft. 9 in.	n.	f.	s.	l.		10	12	13	...	6	10	4	10	...
47	65	Yes	5 ft. 7 in.	l.	s.	f.	n.		8	9	7	...	3	10	1	10	11
48	38	Not	5 ft. 3½ in.	f.	n.	s.	l.		9	10	12	...	5	10	3	20	9
49	15	Yes	5 ft. 3 in.	l.	s.	f.	n.		6	3	3	...	2	8	1	20	...
50	34	Yes	5 ft. 4 in.	n.	f.	s.	l.		9	2	6	...	3	9	1	10	...
51	18	Yes	5 ft. 2 in.	n.	f.	s.	l.		10	11	9	...	3	10	1	13	...
52	50	Not	5 ft. 4½ in.	f.	s.	n.	l.		9	11	11	...	4	10	3	13	...
53	48	Not	5 ft. 5 in.	f.	n.	s.	l.		10	9	11	...	4	10	3	11	18
54	40	Yes	5 ft. 2 in.	l.	s.	f.	n.		10	11	8	...	7	10	7	...	20
55	60	Not	5 ft. 3 in.	l.	s.	f.	n.		8	9	6	...	5	10	3	20	20
56	49	Yes	5 ft. 4 in.	s.	n.	f.	l.		8	6	3	...	4	10	2	14	...
57	46	Yes	5 ft. 2 in.	n.	l.	s.	f.		10	6	4	7	7	10	3	10	...
58	33	Yes	5 ft.	n.	f.	s.	l.		9	3	8	...	5	8	4	20	...
59	22	Yes	5 ft.	n.	s.	f.	l.		7	2	2	...	5	10	6	10	...
60	33	Yes	5 ft. 3 in.	f.	n.	s.	l.		10	10	8	...	4	10	3	15	...
61	21	Yes	5 ft. 7 in.	l.	n.	s.	f.		9	9	5	...	4	10	1	20	20
62	65	Yes	5 ft. 6 in.	n.	f.	l.	s.		11	9	6	...	5	10	1	20	...
63	66	Yes	5 ft. 5 in.	f.	s.	n.	l.		8	10	9	5	9	10	4	15	...
64	26	Yes	5 ft. 6 in.	f.	n.	s.	l.		9	11	11	...	5	10	1	10	...
65	20	Yes	6 ft.	s.	f.	n.	l.		9	9	7	...	5	10	3	10	...
66	13	Yes	4 ft. 4 in.	n.	s.	l.	f.		2	1	1	...	1	0	0	10	0
67	50	Yes	5 ft.	f.	n.	s.	l.		9	10	9	...	5	10	2	12	20
68	26	Yes	5 ft. 6 in.	f.	n.	s.	l.		10	10	10	...	4	10	4	...	...
69	25	Yes	...	...	...	...	...		...	...	...	...	...	...	...	...	...
70	17	Yes	...	...	...	...	...		...	...	...	...	...	...	...	...	...
71	16	Yes	...	...	...	...	...		...	...	...	...	...	...	...	...	...
72	19	Yes	...	...	...	...	...		...	...	...	...	...	...	...	...	...
73	28	Yes	5 ft. 7 in.	f.	n.	s.	l.		9	9	9	...	6	10	3	...	...
74	9	Yes	4 ft. 4 in.	n.	f.	s.	l.		12	6	6	...	5	10	4	8	...
75	30	Yes	...	...	...	...	...		...	...	...	...	...	...	...	14	16
76	12	Yes	3 ft. 4 in.	f.	n.	l.	s.		8	7	3	...	2	10	1	...	...
77	25	Yes	...	...	...	...	...		...	...	...	...	...	...	...	...	20
78	22	Yes	5 ft. 6 in.	s.	f.	n.	l.		9	8	8	...	2	7	1	10	18
79	20	Yes	5 ft. 10 in.	f.	l.	s.	n.		8	8	9	...	3	10	2	10	...
80	12	Yes	4 ft. 8 in.	l.	n.	f.	s.		9	7	9	...	6	10	4	10	...
81	17	Yes	...	...	...	...	...		...	...	...	...	...	...	...	...	...
82	25	Yes	...	...	...	...	...		...	...	...	...	...	...	...	...	...
83	52	Yes	5 ft. 8 in.	f.	n.	s.	l.		8	10	9	...	2	10	1	18	...
84	26	Yes	5 ft. 2 in.	f.	s.	l.	n.		6	7	7	...	4	10	1	18	...
85	18	Yes	4 ft. 0½ in.	f.	s.	n.	l.		7	9	5	...	5	10	3	...	...
86	13	Yes	3 ft. 9 in.	l.	s.	f.	n.		3	1	1	...	1	10	0	11	...
87	21	Yes	5 ft. 7½ in.	l.	s.	f.	n.		8	7	9	10	5	10	4	10	...
88	32	Not	5 ft. 4 in.	s.	f.	n.	l.		7	9	9	12	8	10	6	20	20
89	13	Yes	3 ft. 10 in.	n.	l.	f.	s.		6	2	2	6	2	10	1	8	...
90	15	Yes	4 ft. 8 in.	n.	f.	l.	s.		9	9	5	7	8	10	5	10	...

TABLE NO. I.

Numbers for reference to names in the MSS.	Actual size, by measurement, in inches and tenths.							Development of various parts of the cranium, and activity of various mental faculties, as compared with that of 1000 ordinary persons of the same age and sex; 10 being the standard among ordinary persons.										
	Depth of Chest.	Width of Chest.	Greatest Circumference of Cranium.	Greatest Diameter of Cranium.	Diameter from the root of the Nose to the Occipital Spine.	Transverse Diameter over the Ears	Arc of Cranium from root of Nose to Occipital Spine.	Arc from Ear to Ear.	Size of the Lower Frontal Region.	Skill in the use of the Perceptive Faculties.	Size of the Upper Frontal Region.	Skill in the use of the Reflective Faculties.	Size of the Lateral Region.	Activity of the Faculties of Self-Preservation.	Size of the Posterior Region.	Activity of the Social Attachments.	Size of the Coronal Region.	Activity of the Moral Sentiments.	Size of the Cerebellum.	Activity of the Animal Nature.	Degree of ability to support themselves.
46	8	9	...	7·3	7·3	5·4	...	...	13	4	14	8	6	4	2	6	4	8	5	11	4
47	9·4	11·1	...	8·1	8·1	5·5	...	...	15	4	12	5	9	3	12	6	12	6	11	7	4
48	8·5	9·7	...	7·8	7·8	5·6	...	...	...	4	...	9	...	12	...	7	...	8	...	14	5
49	7·3	9·2	...	7·7	7·7	5·4	...	...	11	2	14	2	11	2	12	4	13	6	5	11	2
50	7·9	10·6	...	8·2	8·2	6	...	...	15	2	16	2	16	1	16	3	14	3	14	8	2
51	7·5	9	...	7·1	7·1	5·4	...	...	10	3	7	8	4	1	1	1	8	2	1	11	3
52	8	10·8	...	7·7	7·7	5·6	...	...	11	4	7	3	7	3	6	1	5	9	5	12	5
53	8·1	10·3	...	8·2	8·1	5·8	...	...	13	8	13	9	11	5	13	10	14	9	10	13	4
54	7·3	10·8	...	7·3	7·3	5·5	...	...	12	7	10	8	7	4	1	6	6	9	4	14	3
55	8·8	10·2	...	7·6	7·6	6·1	...	...	14	4	13	9	14	2	9	3	8	3	6	16	4
56	8	11·1	...	8·2	8·1	5·9	...	...	13	3	12	4	12	2	13	4	14	5	12	8	4
57	7·6	9·6	...	7·8	7·7	6	...	...	13	4	13	8	12	5	9	7	12	5	8	7	4
58	7·5	9·1	...	7·3	7·3	5·1	...	...	5	6	5	6	1	5	5	6	6	7	5	14	5
59	...	...	22	...	...	...	...	...	...	6	...	5	...	4	...	8	...	8	...	6	2
60	7·3	9·2	...	7·5	7·5	5·2	...	...	8	5	2	3	6	3	5	10	1	9	8	11	4
61	8·6	10·3	...	7·7	7·7	5·8	...	...	8	3	11	5	12	3	15	6	12	5	14	15	3
62	9	10·2	...	7·7	7·7	5·6	...	...	6	5	6	5	6	3	10	10	7	6	8	13	3
63	10·8	10·3	22·5	7·7	7·7	5·3	14·5	14·5	...	6	...	4	...	5	...	4	...	3	...	12	5
64	8·4	10·5	...	7·7	7·6	5·4	...	...	6	5	4	4	5	4	9	6	4	7	9	10	5
65	8	11·5	...	7·8	7·7	5·2	...	...	12	4	13	3	6	3	13	8	13	8	5	8	4
66	6·6	8	...	7·6	7·6	5·6	...	...	10	1	10	1	12	4	12	10	10	2	9	3	1
67	7·2	10·7	...	8	8	5·8	...	...	13	5	14	6	13	4	11	3	13	5	8	14	5
68	...	...	...	...	...	...	...	...	...	6	...	5	...	4	...	5	...	8	...	10	5
69	...	...	...	...	...	...	...	...	4	...	3	...	3	...	2	...	2	...	4	3
70	...	...	...	...	...	...	...	...	...	...	...	...	...	...	...	...	...	...	...	...	3
71	...	...	...	...	...	...	...	...	...	...	...	...	...	...	...	...	...	...	...	...	4
72	...	...	...	...	...	...	...	...	5	...	...	...	...	...	...	...	...	...	...	...	5
73	...	...	...	...	...	...	...	...	...	6	...	5	...	4	...	6	...	7	...	8	6
74	...	...	...	...	...	...	...	...	5	...	6	...	6	...	8	...	7	...	8	7	6
75	...	...	...	...	...	...	...	...	...	...	...	...	...	...	...	...	...	...	2	14	4
76	...	...	18	...	...	...	...	...	...	3	...	2	...	1	...	5	...	2	...	3	2
77	...	...	...	...	...	...	...	...	...	...	...	...	...	...	...	...	...	...	...	20	6
78	...	...	...	...	...	...	...	...	...	2	...	3	...	2	...	3	...	2	...	12	2
79	8·8	10·2	...	7·5	7·5	5·7	...	...	10	4	15	6	9	4	10	5	14	8	8	9	5
80	...	...	...	...	...	...	...	...	...	6	...	6	...	5	...	6	...	7	...	9	6
81	...	...	...	...	...	...	...	...	...	...	...	...	...	...	...	...	...	...	...	...	6
82	...	...	...	...	...	...	...	...	...	...	...	...	...	...	...	...	...	...	...	...	5
83	10	11	...	8·3	8·3	5·9	...	...	12	2	10	1	12	2	16	8	10	4	16	13	2
84	6·8	10·9	...	8	8	5·3	...	...	13	3	15	2	12	2	15	4	17	5	8	12	3
85	5·7	7·5	...	6·5	6·5	4·5	...	...	9	6	3	4	·08	5	·5	7	·3	8	·1	5	4
86	8	8·3	...	6·5	6·5	5·4	...	...	...	1	...	0	...	1	...	1	...	0	...	5	0
87	7·6	11	...	8·6	8·6	6	...	...	18	5	18	5	15	4	19	5	20	7	13	9	4
88	10	10·5	22	7·9	7·9	5·4	13	14	14	12	9	6	6	5	5	4	4	6	6	16	6
89	6·4	9·3	...	5·7	5·7	4·3	10·5	11	...	2	...	1	...	1	...	3	...	4	...	5	2
90	6·6	9·3	...	7	7	4·9	...	...	4	7	4	6	·6	4	4	8	4	9	5	7	6

GENERAL SUMMARY OF TABLE No. I.

A.

Showing the actual measurement of Idiotic persons, over 18 years of age, and their comparison with corresponding measurement of 1000 ordinary persons.

		No. of Idiots examined.	Average measurement in inches.	Average measurement of ordinary persons.
Height,	Males,	172	64·7	...
	Females,	116	60·0	...
Depth of chest,	Males,	146	8·0	8·0
	Females,	78	7·3	7·3
Width of chest,	Males,	146	10·0	10·0
	Females,	78	9·3	9·3
Greatest circumference of cranium,	Males,	99	21·7	22·0
	Females,	59	20·7	21·5
Diameter from root of nose to occipital spine,	Males,	94	7·5	7·8
	Females,	87	7·3	7·5
Transverse diameter over the ears,	Males,	94	5·5	5·8
	Females,	87	5·3	5·5
Arc of cranium, from root of nose to occipital spine,	Males,	87	13·3	13·8
	Females,	61	13·0	13·5
Arc from opening of one ear over to opening of the other,	Males,	87	14·0	14·3
	Females,	61	13·5	14·0

B.

Showing the average of certain conditions of body and manifestations of mind in Idiotic persons, compared with similar conditions and manifestations in the average of ordinary persons.

	No. of Idiots examined.	Average of their development.	Average of ordinary persons.
Dynamic condition, or general vigour of body,	504	7·88	10
Tactile sensibility, or general sense of touch,	476	8·52	10
Muscular contractility, or command and direction of muscles,	494	8·33	10
Manifestation of amative feelings,	248	16·5	10
Consumption of food,	444	14·7	10
Sensibility to musical sounds,	300	6·3	10
Skill in the use of language,	452	5	10
Ability to count, or reckon,	461	3	10
Skill in the use of the perceptive faculties,	493	5	10
„ „ reflective „ *	489	3·50	10
Activity of the faculties of self-preservation,	490	4	10
„ social nature, attachment,	479	5	10
„ moral sentiments,*	480	5	10
„ animal nature generally,	504	10	10

* Several cases have been marked 1, 2, or 3, in these columns, upon the supposition that the rudiments of the faculties or sentiments existed, though, on account of physical torpor, they are not manifested. They are generally, perhaps, marked too high.   S. G. H.

C.

Showing the actual development of certain parts of the Cranium in Idiotic persons; the average measurement of the same parts of the Cranium in 1000 ordinary persons; also the activity of certain mental manifestations in the same Idiots, compared with the average activity in ordinary persons.

	No. examined.	Average development and activity in Idiots.	Average development and activity in ordinary persons.
Development of the lower frontal region of the cranium,	116	9	10
Skill in the use of the perceptive faculties,	116	5	10
Development of the upper frontal region of the cranium,	116	9	10
Skill in the use of the reflective or reasoning faculties,	116	3	10
Development of the lateral region of the cranium,	116	8	10
Activity of the faculties of self-preservation, as cautiousness, cunning, &c.,	116	4	10
Development of the posterior region of the cranium,	116	8	10
Activity of the social nature, or attachment to others,	116	6	10
Development of the coronal region of the cranium,	116	9	10
Activity of the moral sentiments,	116	6	10
Development of the region of the cerebellum,	114	7	10
Activity of the amative feelings,	70	14	10
Average activity of the animal nature, estimated by the developments of amative feelings, the dynamic condition of body, and the consumption of food,	115	10	10

TABLE No. 2.

Showing the general condition and capacities of Idiotic persons examined.

	Congenital Idiocy.	Idiocy supervened.	Total.
Whole number of idiotic persons on the roll,	420	154	574
Idiotic persons under 25 years of age,	187	13	200
,, ,, over 25 years of age,	233	141	374
Idiotic persons who are as helpless as infants,	33	20	53
,, ,, ,, ,, as children 2 years old,	43	31	74
,, ,, ,, ,, ,, 7 ,,	73	21	94
,, ,, who can work to some small profit if carefully watched and directed,	110	28	138
,, ,, who can nearly earn their board if directed in work by others,	141	38	179
,, ,, who can earn their board and clothing under the management of discreet persons,	19	17	36
Idiotic persons who have property of their own, and are under guardianship,	20	2	22
,, ,, who belong to wealthy families,	56	6	62
,, ,, who are of poor families, but not public paupers,	196	29	225
,, ,, who are town or state paupers,	148	72	220
,, ,, whose pecuniary condition was not ascertained,	0	45	45
,, ,, who have been countenanced in the practice of masturbation by parents or nurses,	14	5	19
Idiotic persons under 25 years of age who seem capable of improvement,	174	22	196
,, ,, over 25 years of age who seem capable of improvement,	195	97	292
,, ,, under 25 years of age who seem capable of little or no improvement,	13	0	13
,, ,, over 25 years of age apparently capable of little or no improvement,	38	35	73

TABLE No. 3.

Showing the general BODILY *condition of the* 574 *Idiotic persons.*

			Congenital Idiocy.	Idiocy supervened.	Total.
Idiotic persons	with blindness or deformity of the eyes,		15	6	21
,,	,,	with deafness, ...	12	1	13
,,	,,	with deformity of the mouth and nose, .	22	1	23
,,	,,	with deformity of the hands or feet, .	51	3	54
,,	,,	with torpor of feeling, . . .	11	3	14
,,	,,	with paralysis in some or all parts, .	83	13	96
,,	,,	who are insatiably gluttonous, . .	218	62	280
,,	,,	who are known to practise masturbation frequently—			
		Males, . .	59	57	116
		Females, . .	43	32	75
		Total, . .	102	89	191
,,	,,	who are subject to fits, . . .	92	33	125
,,	,,	in whom the use of tobacco at once brings on convulsions, . . .	1	2	3
,,	,,	in whom anger immediately produces violent convulsions and insensibility, .	6	1	7
,,	,,	in whom anger causes spasms and less violent fits, ...	19	3	22
,,	,,	in whom fright causes faintness, nausea, and vomiting, . . .	7	0	7
,,	,,	supposed to have been injured by the use of calomel, ...	0	8	8
,,	,,	supposed to have been injured by the use of opium, ...	0	5	5

TABLE No. 4.

Showing the hereditary tendencies.

	Congenital Idiocy.	Idiocy supervened.	Total.
Idiotic persons who are known to be of decidedly scrofulous families,	355	64	419
,, ,, whose parents were known to be habitual drunkards,	99	15	114
,, ,, some of whose near relatives are idiotic or insane,	177	34	211
,, ,, whose parents were known to be neither very scrofulous nor very intemperate,	5	5	10
,, ,, who have 1 near relative idiotic,	44	5	49
,, ,, ,, 2 ,, ,,	8	1	9
,, ,, ,, 3 ,, ,,	5	1	6
,, ,, ,, 4 ,, ,,	3	1	4
,, ,, ,, 5 ,, ,,	6	0	6
,, ,, ,, 10 ,, ,,	3	0	3
,, ,, ,, 19 ,, ,,	1	0	1
,, ,, one or both of whose parents were idiotic or insane,	...	...	50
,, ,, who are parents,	...	...	21
,, ,, whose parents were advised to marry on account of ill health,	12	0	12
Families where the parents of idiotic persons are near relatives,	17	0	17
Of these families, 6 have 1 idiotic child each	...	...	...
2 ,, 2 ,, children each	...	...	...
3 ,, 3 ,, ,,	...	...	...
5 ,, 4 ,, ,,	...	...	...
1 has 5 ,, ,,	...	...	...
Average idiotic persons in each of these 17 families,	3	0	3
Parents who have 2 idiotic children,	43	2	45
,, ,, 3 ,, ,,	10	3	13
,, ,, 4 ,, ,,	8	0	8
,, ,, 5 ,, ,,	1	0	1
,, ,, 7 ,, ,,	1	0	1
,, ,, 9 ,, ,,	1	0	1
,, ,, 11 ,, ,,	0	1	1
Number of families in which *all* the children born of one marriage were idiotic or very puny, while all those of another marriage, by the surviving *healthy* parent with a healthy person, were sound in body and mind,	...	...	15

TABLE No. 5.

Showing the physical condition of the 574 Idiotic persons.

	Congenital Idiocy.	Idiocy supervened.	Total.
TEMPERAMENTS.			
Idiotic persons in whom the sanguine temperament preponderates,	18	7	25
,, ,, in whom the nervous temperament preponderates,	103	50	153
,, ,, in whom the fibrous temperament preponderates,	110	48	158
,, ,, in whom the lymphatic temperament preponderates,	82	22	104
SIZE, SHAPE, AND CONDITION OF THE HEAD.			
Idiotic persons with hydrocephalic or large heads,	8	1	9
,, ,, with very small heads, among 338 who were measured,	97	2	99
Idiotic persons whose heads were carefully measured with the cephalometer,	100	5	105
Of these 105, there are, of—			
Idiotic persons whose heads are of normal size,	54	4	58
,, ,, whose heads are of both normal size and shape,	29	1	30
,, ,, whose heads are large, but of normal shape,	7	0	7
,, ,, whose heads are very small,	39	0	39
,, ,, whose lower frontal region is preponderating,*	23	0	23
,, ,, whose lower frontal region is deficient,	7	0	7
,, ,, whose upper frontal region is preponderating,	13	0	13
,, ,, whose upper frontal region is deficient,	23	0	23
,, ,, whose lateral region is preponderating,	14	3	17
,, ,, ,, is deficient,	30	1	31
,, ,, whose posterior region is preponderating,	32	2	34
,, ,, ,, is deficient,	24	2	26
,, ,, whose top or coronal region is preponderating,	30	2	32
,, ,, whose top or coronal region is deficient,	16	1	17
,, ,, whose cerebellum is preponderating,	22	2	32
,, ,, ,, is deficient,	43	1	44

* By *preponderating* is meant that the region in question is largely developed in comparison with other regions in the same cranium; not that there is any absolute deformity.

APPENDIX.

No. I.

INFLUENCE OF THE SIZE OF THE BRAIN UPON IDIOCY.

UNDER this head, Dr Howe, in a Report on "Training and Teaching Idiots," made by him to the Governor of Massachusetts in February 1850, introduces the following remarks:—

Owing to causes mentioned in other parts of this report, the variety, not only in mental capacity, but in mental idiosyncracy, is very great among our pupils; not merely as great as among ordinary boys, but far greater. They are, or were at the time of their admission, all of them idiotic; they would have been pronounced so by any person conversant with such cases. Indications of idiocy in all the cases, except those two in which it was complicated with insanity, were so plain as not to be mistaken. Out of the whole number, however, there were only two who would have been recognised as idiots by mere examination of their heads. Taking the whole thirteen together, the average size of their heads is larger than the ordinary size of the heads of persons of their age; but it is to be observed, that one was hydrocephalic. Leaving him out, the average of the others would be about the ordinary size.

The two with small heads would be selected by any one at sight as not having brains enough for the manifestation of common sense, first, because their heads are so much smaller than common heads. If their lungs were as much dwarfed in comparison with the other organs of the body, as their brains are, the functions of respiration could not be carried on with any degree of perfection; the blood could not be *oxygenated* fast enough for the purposes of health.

These cases naturally suggest some physiological remarks upon the effects of size of the brain upon idiocy.

Idiocy is sometimes caused by the smallness of the brain; indeed, the true *type* of the lowest class of idiots is a person whose brain is too small to perform its functions normally. The common notion, however, that this is generally the cause of idiocy, is incorrect. Out of 338 cases, the measurement of which is given by the Massachusetts commissioners, only 99 had diminutive brains. Among our boys, only two have very diminutive brains.

The size of the brain which is necessary for a normal manifestation of intellect, varies according to the quality and condition of the bodily organization, as will be shown presently.

When the idiocy arises, as it probably does in the majority of cases, from some congenital imperfection in the organization of the brain, or from some inherited tendency to deranged action, then the variety in the appearance and in the condition of the sufferers, is almost as great as is their number. They have heads of the ordinary size, or, perhaps, even larger than usual. They are uncouth in their appearance, and strange in their ways; they are often deformed or distorted; they appear to have the rudiments of all the parts or attributes of man, but these are so disproportioned, and so ill adapted to each other, that it seems a hopeless task to make out of them a harmonious whole. Idiots of this class, however, preserve the human appearance. Disfigured and even distorted as they are, they still seem human; they are like men, and not animals, in their looks.

When, however, the idiocy arises from insufficient size of brain, the idiot generally loses the peculiarly human appearance, and sinks to the likeness of the higher animals in his looks and actions.

My observations have not yet perhaps been sufficiently extensive to give much importance to this suggestion, but it seems to be made more probable by *a priori* reasoning. Organic defect or functional derangement may affect *any* part of the brain, and the idiocy that follows may be from want of harmonious action among the faculties; and this want of harmony will manifest itself in a thousand different ways, for there are thousands and tens of thousands of possible inharmonious actions among so many functions and faculties, and only one harmonious action.

When the brain is merely too small, then, if it is dwarfed equally in all its parts, we should expect to see a very feeble but a harmonious development of character; the feebleness might be so great as to amount to idiocy, but we should have a man in miniature. This, however, is not the case; at least, it is not, so far as my observations have gone. Where the brain is too small, it is not dwarfed equally in all its parts, but it is especially so in the upper and forward region,—in the parts which are considered by many physiologists, as the seat of the organs of the peculiarly human faculties and sentiments; while the hinder and lower parts of the brain, or those supposed to be the seat of the organs of the appetites and propensities common to men and animals, are far less affected. Nature first makes sure of those parts necessary to the continuance of the individual and of the race, as the foundations without which there can be no superstructure. The lower or animal region of the brain predominating in size, not only renders the person more active in his animal nature, but gives to him a peculiarly animal look.

It should ever be remembered that this disproportion between the different parts of the brain, though small at first, will constantly increase, not only in the idiot, but in every one, if left unchecked by proper means. That which is by nature a little the strongest becomes, by *exercise of its functions*, and by *neglect of exercise* of the functions of other parts, *very much* the *strongest*, until it utterly prostrates and masters them. Hence the high duty and responsibility of the more gifted to the less gifted; hence the claim of the idiot and of the youth of low organization upon the men of high organization,—a claim stronger even than that of ordinary youth; for these are they who have terrible wars in their members, and who are not, and cannot be, a law unto themselves.

May not the organic peculiarities, the instincts, habits, and appearances of idiots,—true idiots,—give us some clue to the process of development of the race of mankind?

In all the early steps of the great progress hitherto made by the human race, the lower or animal parts of our nature have been more active than the higher ones, except in the rare cases of richly-gifted men, who have risen up from time to time, and stood like prophets, showing the capacity, and foretelling the elevation of man. During all this time the improvement of the bodily organization has preceded and influenced the improvement in character. The farther we go back towards the barbarous condition, the lower we find the organic condition of the people to be. Those tribes which still linger behind in savagedom show us the race not yet emerged from its youth, by reason of the great comparative activity of the animal propensities.

Now it seems as if the dwarfed brain of the idiot shows us a still earlier and lower condition; it exhibits the animal man still more clearly, and shows him to resemble the monkey most closely in his looks. It is not merely the *up-looking* and twinkling eye, the flattened forehead, the projecting jaws, and the other anatomical peculiarities that give him this likeness, but sometimes, moreover, the likeness is seen in habits and actions. One of our pupils, besides all the marks just mentioned, which give him a strong likeness to the monkey, has, moreover, the long arms of the ape; he moves about with his head and shoulders stooping, and his arms hanging forward, as though he were going to drop upon all fours. One of his pleasures is to climb upon a desk or high place, and leap through the air, with outstretched limbs, upon some one's neck, and to cling around him, not as a common child does, with his arms alone, but twining his legs about him as though he were one of the Quadrumana.

There are many remarkable instances on record of idiotic persons manifesting a striking likeness in their habits to the habits of the higher animals; and if it be found, as I think it will, that this likeness is strongest in those who have very small brains, then we may suspect, not only that their idiocy is caused by diminutive size of the brain, but that there has been a progressive development of that organ in the progress of the race. Some of these habits seem to show the reappearance of instincts which could only have belonged to man in a low animal condition, and which have entirely died out in the race long ago, even before it arrived at savagedom. Such, for instance, is the gnawing off the umbilical cord of the infant by an idiotic mother, in the manner of animals.

Some of the cases in our school furnish interesting evidence in support, not only of the doctrine that diminutive size of brain may cause idiocy, but, moreover, that the texture or *quality* of its organic tissue may modify very materially the manifestations of mind made through it. There is a certain point as to bulk, below which, if the brain falls, the person must necessarily be idiotic; but that point varies very much in different individuals, as was said just now, and depends upon or is connected with those conditions of the bodily organization comprehended under the term *temperament*. The most important of these conditions seems to be, that of the tissue of the fibres of the body, especially that of the brain and nervous system. This may be recognised by external marks, by the hair, features, skin, proportion of the limbs, and appearance of *fineness* or coarseness in the texture of the body generally. It is easily known when once observed. It is the true standard of beauty. The perfection of it is best expressed by the single word *blood*, or high blood. There is very great difference among men in this respect; the vessel of fine porcelain excels not more in beauty, and especially in fineness of grain, the coarse earthen jug, than does a man of blood, or high temperament, excel one of low and coarse organization;

no matter though the first be a North American Indian, the second a prince whose

> " Ancient but ignoble blood
> Has crept through scoundrels ever since the flood."

As the Arabian steed is to the cart-horse, so is the man of fine temperament to the man of coarse temperament.

This difference in temperament, and the effects of it, are seen in two of the idiot boys mentioned above. The cranium of the first, G. Rowell, measures 14·91 inches in its greatest circumference, 10·44 inches from ear to ear over the top of the head, and 10·13 inches from the root of the nose to the occipital spine.

The head of the second, Edmund, measures 17·06 inches in its greatest circumference, 11·07 from ear to ear, and 11·75 from the root of the nose to the occipital spine. It is fair to conclude, then, that in both these cases the idiocy arises from want of sufficient bulk of brain; indeed, the first falls short of the size supposed to be necessary for manifestation of any intellect by physiologists who have written upon the subject.

The first-named boy, whose head is so much smaller than the second, and, indeed, than any boy in the school, and who has such a striking resemblance to the ape tribe, manifests much more vivacity, activity, and intelligence than the second, and, indeed, than several of the others. He is very active, very resolute, and very passionate. He masters all the boys who are anywhere near his own age, and sometimes strives for the mastery over the bigger ones.

Now, why is it that of these boys whose idiocy is caused by want of bulk of brain, the one with the smallest brain should manifest the most intelligence and the most character? Precisely for the reason that the man of "blood," or fine temperament, is superior in these respects to the man of coarse organization, though his brain may be smaller; for the same reason that the Arabian steed is superior to the cart-horse, not only in fleetness, but also in sagacity. This boy's body is of a much finer organization, and his brain, doubtless, is so likewise. In his bodily structure generally the nervous system has a greater comparative development than in the second, who is rather of the lymphatic temperament. His features are more cleanly cut and chiselled, his skin is softer and more delicate, his hair is finer, his eyes are more lively and fiery, his limbs are more delicately shaped, his fingers are longer, and differ more from each other in length. As compared with the other, he is more of what may be called the poetic temperament; he is an idiot, but an idiot made of *finer clay*, and in a finer mould.

As a small machine—say a mill—if made of fine material and well constructed, may turn out more meal than a larger one of coarse materials rudely put together; so a small and fine brain may do more *thinking* than a bulky and coarse one. But let not the sceptic lose sight of the rest of the figure: there can be no mill built without a BUILDER, and it can turn out no meal at all without a *miller!*

It is interesting to examine these boys with a view to the faculty which they manifest for speech. They were both in good health when they entered, they were pretty free and active in their motions, and had, for idiots, very good command of most of the voluntary muscles. The senses, especially those of sight and hearing, were tolerably active, but they could not speak a word. That part of natural language which we call the language of signs, which expresses certain emotions, and which men have in common with the higher animals, was possessed by these boys in about as much perfection as it is by trained monkeys and dogs; but the peculiarly human attribute, speech, was utterly wanting. Nevertheless, the difference between the man, even in his lowest or animal state, and the brute, was clearly visible in these boys, and seemed to be a difference, not in degree, *but in kind.* They had no speech; they could not make the simplest sentence; but they had the germs of the *capacity* and of the *disposition* to speak,—not as the parrot speaks—not to imitate sounds merely—but to attach *names* or vocal sounds to things, and to use these sounds as *the signs of the things.* They have therefore the natural disposition and capacity to form language—attributes which are utterly wanting even in the highest animals, and for lack of which none of them ever can be made to use it.

Both these boys have learned a number of words, and take great pleasure in using them. It is a most touching sight to see the efforts which poor little Edmund makes to repeat over the words that he has learned, and to show to every one whom he meets that he understands them. There seems to be a human soul struggling to free itself from a brutish form, into which, by some magic, it had been metamorphosed. He goes about holding up a nail, a stick, a ball, or any object of which he has learned the name, and, presenting it before the eyes of every one whom he meets, he strives to pronounce the name clearly, and repeat it over, as if he would challenge attention, and proclaim his title to a share of human nature. He has not, perhaps, learned as many words as a parrot might have learned in the same time, but his words are to him names of things,—signs by which his unfledged spirit may interchange signals with the strong-winged spirits about him; for, idiot as

APPENDIX. 65

he is, he is a human being, and language is already to him what it never can be to the most loquacious parrot that ever lived,—it is a medium for the conveyance of his simple thought, and for his understanding the thought of others.

No. II.

RESULTS OF THE EXPERIMENTAL SCHOOL FOR TEACHING AND TRAINING IDIOTIC CHILDREN IN MASSACHUSETTS. (Extracted from the Third and Final Report on the School, by Dr S. G. Howe, 1852.)

Of the whole number of pupils of whom account is to be made, four, the youngest of whom was about six years of age, could not sit erect, and had no use of their limbs when they entered the school; they could not even put victuals to their mouths. Two of these only proved to be proper subjects, and remained. They have both greatly improved: they can sit up at a desk or table, and one can use his legs and toddle about by holding on to the wall.

Seven had very imperfect use of their limbs. They could walk about a room feebly, but could not help themselves. Of these seven, four only remained; and of these four, three have greatly improved; the other has not.

Seventeen were filthy in their habits. Of these, thirteen have greatly improved. Most of them are now habitually clean, and always desirous of being so. The other four have as yet made little improvement.

Twenty-two could not dress themselves. Of the twelve who remained over a year, eight now dress themselves without assistance.

Of the whole twenty-eight, twenty-one could not feed themselves. Of these twenty-one, eleven only were retained more than a year, but all of these save one have greatly improved in this respect.

With regard to intellectual condition, eighteen were dumb, or used only a few detached words in an interjectional sense,— as Mamma! Of these, only ten remained. Four now talk, that is, use more or less words with meaning; two begin to do so; and four are still mute.

Four used single words. Three only of these remained, and

E

of the three, two now put their words into sentences. The third has improved.

Five of the whole could make and use simple sentences. Four have remained, and have greatly improved in the use of speech.

Of the whole number, only four knew their letters. Of the remaining twenty-four, only twelve remained over a year. Of these twelve, eight now know their letters and can make out single sentences, and some can *read* simple stories.

It is true that these children and youth speak and read but little, and that little very imperfectly compared with others of their age; but if one brings the case home, and supposes these to be his own children, it will not seem a small matter that a daughter, who it was thought would never know a letter, can now read a simple story, and a son, who could not say father, can now distinctly repeat a prayer to his Father in heaven.

It may be said of the whole, saving only those who proved to be deranged in intellect, that they are more tidy in person and habits, more active in their movements, more intelligent, and more capable of being made useful, than when they entered the school.

Such are some of the results of the Experimental School for teaching and training Idiotic Children, as far as they can be set forth in numbers and words; but, as was observed before, the principal result, being of a moral nature, cannot well be so set forth. . . . .

When men estimate the products of an investment in banks or manufactures, they look to the balance-sheet, and ask for the dividends. But not so should they do in estimating the value of institutions of beneficence. Not so have the generous people in the country, and the munificent merchants in the cities of Massachusetts, estimated the returns of their vast investment in charitable institutions for the relief of the unfortunate; nor will they so estimate the value of what has been done for the most pitiable and helpless of all the children of misfortune,—the poor idiots. It is not so they will measure the value of the sense of relief and hope to the parents and friends of these children,—the feeling of comfort and pleasure to the children themselves,—the worth, the moral worth, of an honest effort in their behalf to those immediately concerned in the work, and to the whole community that employs them.

He who should attempt to set forth and compare the profit and the loss to Massachusetts of her State Lunatic Asylum, and should leave out of the account the moral gain to the community, would show a sad lack of moral perception.

Is not the moral and religious sense of the people quickened and increased by building up and sustaining that noble establishment? It has taken poor wretches who were confined and chained in cellars, in garrets, or in cages—who were objects of dread, and the habitual sight of whose degradation demoralized the beholders; it has made these the subjects of its tender care. Has it not thus increased men's respect for God, by teaching them to respect all who are made in his image? Has it not thus been teaching daily lessons of mercy and humanity? Nay, does it not—now that the people once so indifferent to the fate of the poor lunatic have learned their duty to him—does it not whisper another lesson, and bid them learn their duty to the poor idiot also? And does not a people which gains a new sense of duty to humanity thereby gain a new source of spiritual riches?

It would be possible, perhaps, to convince even those who have no faith in any but tangible results, if they could only be made to put their fingers into the wounds and examine the matter, that in no way can the education of idiots be all loss. It would be easy to show, that while idiots are neglected, they are lazy, idle, destructive, and of course very expensive; whereas, if they are properly taught and trained to industry, a few of them will support themselves by their work, many of them will contribute something towards their own support, and almost all of them become less burdensome and expensive. But it is not necessary to urge these secondary considerations. It will suffice to repeat, that the result of these three years of trial has proved that many idiots are capable of being greatly improved in their bodily habits, in their mental capacities, and even in their spiritual natures; and almost all can be made less burdensome to their friends and the community.

No. III.

Institution of the Massachusetts School for Idiotic and Feeble-Minded Youth.

The success of the experiment in the Institution for the Blind induced the Legislature to pass an act in 1850, incorporating a permanent School. At the same time it was resolved, that there be paid annually, out of the treasury of the Commonwealth, to the treasurer of the school, the sum of 5000 dollars, to be devoted to teaching and training indigent idiotic children belonging to the Commonwealth. Among the conditions annexed to this grant, it is provided that the Institution shall gratuitously receive and educate thirty idiotic persons, to be designated by the Governor; and that other applicants of proper age and condition, children of inhabitants of the Commonwealth who are not wealthy, shall be received at a charge not exceeding the actual average cost of the inmates.

No. IV.

PROGRESS OF THE MASSACHUSETTS SCHOOL FOR IDIOTIC AND FEEBLE-MINDED YOUTH. (Extracted from Dr Howe's Seventh Annual Report, 1855.)

The School had its origin in that feeling of respect for humanity, which is pained by the thought that any who bear its image are left unembraced in the common bond of brotherly love, and outcast from the common family, however low in the scale, or however deformed and infirm they may be.

This feeling lies deep in the hearts of the people of Massachusetts, and has never been appealed to in vain, whether for the insane, the deaf, the blind, or the infirm of any class; and it led the Legislature promptly to embrace the idiot in the circle of the State's bounties, when asked to do so.

There was no question about cost and return. There was no hesitation arising from the prevailing belief that idiots must always remain idiots. There they stood,—their infirmity their only claim; but that claim was admitted instantly, and all the more readily because of their own inability to urge it. Be their chance for improvement greater or less, still they were human, and, as such, entitled to every possible opportunity and aid for developing to the utmost their capacity for knowledge, virtue, and happiness.

Such were the feelings and views of those who, nine years ago, asked the Legislature of Massachusetts to ascertain the number and condition of the idiots of the Commonwealth, and, two years afterwards, to provide for their proper care and instruction; and such was the spirit in which they were met. Provision was made immediately for an experimental school,

APPENDIX. 69

which, proving successful, was made a permanent one, and to which additional aid was granted. That school has now been in uninterrupted and successful operation more than seven years. During all this time it has been properly a State School, because the State provided the principal means for its existence. That existence has not been the less real, or less historical, because the establishment has been carried on in a building not expressly constructed for it. It is a shallow notion that wood and stone, put together in a particular form, constitute an institution, or even its essential features.

During all this time, the school has been performing its work of beneficence, and its effects have been felt at home and abroad. Not only was the public heart and conscience quickened and improved by making an effort in behalf of these unfortunates, as a matter of manifest duty, though with ever so small prospect of success; but a conviction was produced in the minds of thousands who had despaired of any good practical results, that those results were most evident and valuable. The conviction is becoming common in Massachusetts, that idiots are educable to a considerable extent; and the duty of providing for their instruction and training at the public expense is generally admitted.

This change has not been effected here alone, but it has extended to other States. In New York, where Dr Baccus had been the early, able, and zealous champion of the cause, the Legislature, which he had earnestly but vainly urged to make provision for a school for idiots, was at last prevailed upon to do so, mainly in consequence of an exhibition in their hall of pupils from our school.

The following letter from the Hon. Christopher Morgan, then Secretary of the Board of Education, is an interesting historical document :—

Albany, March 23, 1852.

DEAR SIR,—I remember with great satisfaction your visit to Albany with the idiotic pupils under your charge. Previous to your visit, I had regarded the institutions for the instruction of idiots rather as asylums for the improvement of the physical condition of the idiots, than for educational purposes.

A very attentive examination of your pupils convinced me that their physical defects might be in a great measure remedied, and their minds cultivated and enlarged to an extent far beyond anything I had imagined.

The exhibition before the Legislature was eminently satisfactory and convincing.

Dr Baccus, recently a State Senator, and an enlightened and philanthropic citizen of Rochester, laboured with zeal and fidelity, though unsuccessfully, to establish an institution for idiots in this State. Very soon after your visit to Albany, a law was passed for the establishment of an institution for idiots ; an appropriation of six thousand dollars a year, for two years, was made, and the Institution is now in successful operation in the vicinity of the city, under the judicious management of Dr Wilbur.

It may now be regarded as permanently established, and to your visit, more than anything else, are we indebted for this noble charity, so creditable to the liberality and benevolence of the State.—Very respectfully and truly yours,

CHRISTOPHER MORGAN.

To the Superintendent of the School for
Idiotic Children, Boston, Mass.

The New York School was organized very soon after at Albany, and put under the charge of a citizen of Massachusetts, Dr Wilbur, who had gained valuable experience in a private school for imbecile children, founded and conducted by himself. He conducted the New State School with eminent ability and success. In consequence of this success, the State has made generous provision for the permanency of the institution, by laying the foundations of a large and commodious edifice at Syracuse, to be devoted for ever to the training and teaching of idiotic children.

In Pennsylvania, too, the impulse has been felt. Another citizen of Massachusetts, Mr J. B. Richards, who had been the successful teacher of our Experimental School, went thither and devoted himself to the cause. A school has been established there, which will doubtless soon grow into a large and permanent State institution.

Rhode Island, too, has recognised the claims of the idiot to participation in the common blessing of instruction, and made provision for sending some to this school.

The impulse thus given will not stop here. It will be felt in other States and communities, and they will recognise the Christian duty, not only in providing nurture for the ninety-and-nine, but also of going out to seek the one that has so long been lost, and great shall be the joy over its recovery.

Such are some of the general effects of the establishment and existence of this school. The more particular ones may be briefly stated.

One hundred and thirteen pupils have been admitted to the

school since its commencement in 1848, of whom forty-one still continue under its charge.

It has been absolutely necessary to limit the number of pupils, according to the ability of the Institution to provide for them; and accordingly many who have sought admission have not yet found it. The aim has been, so far as is possible, to admit those whose age and condition gave chance for improvement. Nevertheless, as it is difficult in many cases, and impossible in some, to ascertain at first sight whether a child is capable of improvement, a wide door has been opened, and some admitted with but little hope of their being retained. On ascertaining the existence of confirmed insanity, or epilepsy, or other disorders which are beyond the reach of the curative means possessed by the Institution, such children have been discharged to make room for other and more improvable cases.

The chief objects aimed at have been—First, to put the pupils into the best possible condition of health and vigour; to develop strength and activity of body; and to train them to the command and use of muscle and limb. Second, to check inordinate animal appetites; to correct unseemly habits; to accustom them to temperance, cleanliness, and order; and to strengthen their powers of self-control, so that they may be at least less unsightly or disagreeable to others. Third, to train them to some habits of industry, so that they may be at least less burdensome to others in after life. Fourth, to develop as far as possible their mental faculties and moral sentiments, by exercises and lessons suitable to their feeble condition and capacities, and thus to elevate them in the scale of humanity.

With a few there has been no noticeable success in any of these respects; but this was because the idiocy was complicated, and aggravated by morbid activity of brain, or by other grave disorders of the system. With the great majority, however, there has been marked and gratifying success in the attainment of these objects. In some cases, the change in the appearance, condition, and habits of the children has been so great as to amount almost to a new creation. From sickly, gluttonous, stupid, and slothful creatures, they have become healthy, self-controlling, active, and comparatively bright children and youth. Some have been rescued from the category of idiocy, into which they had fallen by reason of disease, neglect, or unfavourable circumstances, rather than been born to it. Others have been so far improved as to become inoffensive even to the most fastidious persons, and to be capable of earning their livelihood under the care of kind and judicious friends.

If there has been any disappointment with respect to the

degree of mental improvement which is attainable by idiotic children as a class, there has been none at all with regard to a number of individual cases. As to the capacity for general improvement in bodily condition and appearance, in personal habits, and capacity for usefulness, there has not only been no disappointment, but, on the contrary, more than full gratification of all expectations, and even hopes. This is put beyond all question by the testimony of numerous relatives and friends of the pupils, and by that of careful observers of the school.

In one respect the result has been unexpected,—namely, the more positive and marked advantage which the school has been to girls than to boys. The natural gentleness of the sex makes them more submissive, more docile, more ready to renounce bad habits, while they are more imitative and more desirous of pleasing. Then their greater fitness for sedentary and household life and duties qualifies them for usefulness in a sphere which boys cannot fill.

The Experimental School was for boys only; and perhaps this was well, for success with them was a sure guarantee of greater success with girls. Experience shows, moreover, that it will be wise to give greater attention to mechanical operations, and less to mere school exercises, than was originally contemplated.

[In his Report for 1856, Dr Howe says:—]

The experience of the past year, in our school, confirms that of former years, and shows the rule to be, that young idiots have great capacity for improvement in their bodily condition, in their habits, manners, minds, and morals, and that the exceptions to it are very few. Even these few, however, if better understood and more skilfully treated, might prove to be no exceptions to the law of improvability of all created beings, during their period of growth and development; or they might reveal a provisional and merciful clause in the law—to wit, that where the original defect or supervened derangement of the organization is so great as utterly to pervert the main functions of life, then a process of decay sets in and forbids the being from long cumbering the ground.

We know that other provisions of the kind exist, as where mechanical injury of some great organ prevents the performance of functions essential to the well-being of other organs, when decay at once begins and death soon follows.

We know also, that in those cases of idiocy where defective organization or deep-seated disease reveals itself in severe and frequent epilepsy, or other affections indicating such shocks of the brain and nervous system as necessarily bar their functions, then the days of the sufferer are soon cut short. Nature will not be utterly defeated, but prefers dissolution to entire perversion of the purposes for which the union of parts into a whole was made.

No. V.

RELATION OF POVERTY TO INSANITY AND IDIOCY. (Extracted from a Report on Insanity and Idiocy in Massachusetts, by the Commission on Lunacy, under resolve of the Legislature of 1854.)*

There is manifestly a much larger ratio of the insane among the poor, and especially among those who are paupers, than among the independent and more prosperous classes.

In this connection it is worth while to look somewhat at the nature of poverty, its origin, and its relation to man and to society. It is usually considered as a single outward circumstance—the absence of worldly goods; but this want is a mere incident in this condition—only one of its manifestations. Poverty is an inward principle, enrooted deeply within the man, and running through all his elements; it reaches his body, his health, his intellect, and his moral powers, as well as his estate. In one or other of these elements it may predominate, and in that alone he may seem to be poor; but it usually involves more than one of the elements, often the whole. Hence we find that, among those whom the world calls poor, there is less vital force, a lower tone of life, more ill health, more weakness, more early death, a diminished longevity. There are also less self-respect, ambition and hope, more idiocy and insanity, and more crime, than among the independent.

The preponderance of mental defect and disease among the poor is unquestionably shown by the comparison of the number of lunatics and idiots in the two classes. None could for a moment suppose that the total of these classes, the independent and the pauper, are in this ratio.

The whole number of permanent and temporary paupers

* The Commissioners were, Edward Jarvis, M.D., of Dorchester, Mass.; Levi Lincoln; and Increase Sumner. Dr Jarvis was the chief conductor in the investigations, and the Report was drawn by him. To this able physician and statistical writer the editors of the present pamphlet are indebted for all the American documents which have contributed to its contents.

74   APPENDIX.

who were relieved or supported from the public treasury in Massachusetts, during the last year (1854), was 23,125. At the same time the calculated population of the State was 1,124,676, of whom 1,102,551 were independent and self-supporting. These are in the ratio of one to forty-seven, whereas the lunatics are in the ratio of 72·9 independent to 100 paupers. Comparing these ratios, we find that the pauper class furnishes, in ratio of its numbers, sixty-four times as many cases of insanity as the independent class.

A similar law of distribution prevails in England and Wales. The pauper lunatics are stated to be 16,821, and those of the independent classes amount to somewhat over 8000,* making the ratio of the pauper to the independent insane about two to one. The ratio of the pauper to the independent classes in the whole population of the kingdom was about as one to twenty, showing the proportion of lunacy among the poor to be about forty times as great as that among those who were not supported by public charity. Whatever reasonable allowance may be made for the defect in the report of the independent lunatics, it is very plain that the ratio of insanity among the paupers is very much larger than that among the self-sustaining class.

This is not only a demonstrable fact in Massachusetts and Great Britain, and probably elsewhere, but it proceeds out of a principle which is fixed in the law of our being—that poverty is not a single fact of an empty purse, but involves in various degrees the whole man, and presents as many facts as there are elements of our nature that can be depreciated or perverted. Insanity is, then, a part and parcel of poverty ; and wherever that involves any considerable number of persons, this disease is manifested.

It needs no philosophy to show that some, perhaps many lunatics, by their disease lose their power of self-sustenance, and are thereby removed from the independent to the pauper class. The labouring but self-supporting poor, whose daily and monthly toil yields barely sufficient for their nourishment, gather no store and gain no capital to rest upon when production is suspended. Of course, when they cease to be producers, they become dependent on others for their support; and this is the more inevitable when that cause is sickness, which cuts off the supply, and creates the necessity of a greater expenditure. In these families the income of the day is only sufficient for its ordinary support, and will bear no more burden. Any increase, then, of expense, must diminish the comfort or the sustenance which was before deemed necessary, or make a demand upon their friends or the public for support.

* Report of Commissioners in Lunacy, 1844, p. 7.

When the poor become thus sick and dependent, although friends may, in some instances, be able and willing to step in and meet this expense, yet unfortunately they, too, are generally poor, and the public treasury is the only and the necessary resort for help; and especially when any one becomes insane, the town or the State necessarily assumes the burden. Moreover, as this disease, more than others, is lasting, it would more certainly exhaust any little gathered store of the poor, and the power and the patience of friends; and then, if the lunatic is not at once thrown upon the public, he must ultimately reach that end.

Besides all this, the difficulty of keeping a lunatic in the dwellings and families of the poor is great and insurmountable. They have no spare room to keep him, and no surplus strength or help to attend upon him, for all of these are appropriated to the irresistible wants of the household from day to day. For this and the preceding reason, any subordinate member of a poor family becoming insane must be sent to the poorhouse or the hospital, to be supported and cared for by the public treasury, and thus become a pauper, at least through the period of the insanity, while yet the rest of the family support themselves. It necessarily follows, that some lunatics are paupers, while their families are yet independent. Therefore, in determining the ratio of lunatics to their respective constituent classes, it is not a safe method to divide the whole number of the paupers, sane and insane, by the number of lunatics among them, because all these who have just been described as coming from self-supporting, although poor families, must be assumed to represent those who are not paupers, and are not included in the pauper class.*

Nevertheless, even if all the self-sustaining poor were included with the paupers in the calculation, there will unquestionably be found a much greater ratio of lunatics among them than among the classes more favoured in respect to outward estate.

A careful examination of the causes of poverty and lunacy, and of the character and condition and health of the poor, would lead to the inference that there would be an excess of lunacy among them.

It may be supposed, from what has been already said, that much of poverty has a common origin with insanity. Both of

* The Report of the Paupers of Massachusetts for the year ending November 1, 1854, published by the Secretary of State, shows that 925 of those relieved or supported became pauper by reason of insanity or idiocy.

them grow out of and represent internal mental character, or physical condition, as well as external circumstances.

Men of unbalanced mind and uncertain judgment do not see the true nature and relation of things, and they manifest this in the management of their common affairs. They do not adapt the means which they possess or use to the ends which they desire to produce. Hence they are unsuccessful in life; their plans of obtaining subsistence for themselves or their families, or of accumulating property, often fail; and they are consequently poor, and often paupers.

This unbalanced and ill-regulated mind, and these wayward or loose habits of thought, are among the common causes of insanity.

The weak mind cannot grasp any complicated design in affairs, nor combine means to produce ends, nor lay and carry out plans of business; the unstable mind changes its purposes, and does not carry out its plans, however well laid. Both of these fail of securing worldly prosperity, and often bring on poverty and pauperism, and they also often produce insanity. People of this class falter beneath the struggles and trials of life, and disappointments bear them down. Their minds become more and more unbalanced and irregular, and at length disordered.

Likewise some physical causes have their doubly destructive influence upon both the estate and the mind.

Intemperance in stimulating drinks, and all sorts of dissipation, disturb and exhaust the brain, and affect its power of correct and ready action; and hence the mind becomes wayward, its operations uncertain, and unfitted for the business of life. Hence follow derangements in the affairs of the world, and ill success and poverty. Hence, too, follow disorders of the nervous system and insanity, which, according to hospital records, find their most common origin in the exciting and exhausting effects of alcohol, especially among the poor.

Whatever depreciates the vital energies lowers the tone of the muscles, and diminishes the physical force, and lessens thereby the power of labour and of production; it also lowers the tone of the brain and the capacity of self-management. In this state the cerebral organ struggles, and may be deranged; consequently we find in the hospital records that ill health is one of the most commonly assigned causes of insanity. It has its first depressing effect on the energy of physical action and the soundness of the judgment in worldly affairs, and next on the power and discipline of the mental faculties.

Among the paupers, eighty-six per cent. are shown to be

incurable; while among those of the independent class a smaller proportion, seventy-five per cent., are returned as beyond hope of restoration. It is not to be supposed that pecuniary pauperism is in itself more destructive to the vital forces which would overcome disease and restore the balance of mental action when the brain is disordered; but the cause of the incurableness and permanence of their mental derangement lies behind, and is anterior to, their outward poverty. The permanence of the disease is often the cause of destitution. They are both frequently traceable to the same source; for an imperfectly organized brain and feeble mental constitution not only carry with them the inherent elements of poverty and insanity, but they have insufficient recuperative power to regain even their original health when deranged, and therefore their disorder remains.

In some cases, the family of an insane patient, although independent, are unable to pay the expenses of his support at an hospital. They have a becoming self-respect which will not permit them to ask for aid from the public, and yet they are too poor to furnish the means of restoration themselves; consequently the lunatic is neglected, and his malady suffered to become chronic and hopeless. His family maintain him at home until both their means and his chance of recovery are exhausted; and then he is sent to the poorhouse, and at once swells the list of incurable paupers.

In other cases, the families of the poor and those of small estates make extraordinary exertions, and support an insane member at the hospital as long as the disorder seems to be curable; but when it becomes fixed and past remedy, their strength gives out and their courage fails, their pride is overcome, and then they allow their relative to become a public charge. In these cases, the incurability alone is the cause of the pauperism.

No. VI.

CAUSES OF IDIOCY, REPORTED BY THE COMMISSIONERS ON IDIOCY TO THE GENERAL ASSEMBLY OF CONNECTICUT, MAY 1856. (Extracted from their Report, p. 9.)

Over one-fifth of the whole number reported are paupers; of the others a large number are in indigent circumstances.

Seventeen families have been reported in which there were more than one idiot. In these seventeen families there were fifty-one idiots, being an average of three to each family. In two cases there were five in one family.

Our statistics of causes, so far as reported, are believed to be reliable; 310 out of 531 reported an adequate cause. Of these causes, following the order of the tables, we find consanguinity of parents to have been a probable cause in twenty cases; epilepsy in seventy-six; self-abuse in nineteen; vicious habits of parents in ninety-five out of 235 cases reported, and of these intemperance specified in seventy-six, and this existing with both parents in thirty cases; with the father alone in forty-three cases, and the mother alone in three.

Feeble condition of one or both parents was a probable cause in thirty-three cases of 163 reported. Deficient mental capacity in one or both parents, in sixty-five out of 185 cases reported. Tendencies to consumption, scrofula, or eruptive disease, was a possible cause in forty-one cases of 145 reported.

The existence of idiocy, insanity, epilepsy, blindness, or melancholy, on the part of one or both parents, was a probable cause in seventy of 164 cases reported.

The mother was subjected to fright or grief during the period of gestation in fifty-three of 108 cases reported.

There are two or three towns in the State in which there are families of idiots, in which parents and children are all imbecile. In one instance, where a pauper female idiot lived in one town, the town authorities hired an idiot belonging to another town, and not then a pauper, to marry her, and the result has been that the town to which the male idiot belongs, has for many years had to support the pair, and three idiot children.

In one instance, where three children had been idiots, they had been kept by their unnatural mother in a close room, in the most filthy condition possible, tied with a short rope around their necks, and never suffered to stand, or to take the fresh air; neighbours and others had remonstrated, but in vain. It is not surprising that under this treatment two of the three had died. It was surprising that they lived to adult age.

No. VII.

Schools in Great Britain for the Education of Idiots.

London School, } *Secretary*—Mr William Nichols,
Colchester School, } 29 Poultry, London.

Lowestoft School.—Private Training Institution for Imbecile Children, Colville House, near Lowestoft.—Proprietor, Dr Foreman.

Salisbury School.—Trinity Sanitary College, for Idiots exclusively of the Higher Class, at "the Hill," Laverstock, Salisbury. The direction of this establishment is under James Abbott, M.A., author of "The Handbook of Idiocy."

Bath School.—*Secretary*, Miss Ranking, 35 Belvidere, Bath.

Edinburgh School, 10 Gayfield Square.—*Resident Superintendents*, Dr and Mrs Brodie.

Dundee School, at Baldovan, near the town.— *Physician*, Dr Gibson, Dundee.

Reports have been published by the Directors of all or some of these Schools; and in 1856 an instructive pamphlet was printed by Dr Brodie, on "The Education of the Imbecile, and the Improvement of Invalid Youth," 8vo, pp. 20. It concludes as follows:—

"From the history of this movement, as sketched in the preceding pages, we think the following deductions may be legitimately drawn:—

"1. That very many, perhaps a majority of children, born with such defects of the nervous system as issue in idiocy or imbecility, are susceptible of great improvement, both in mind and body, under appropriate treatment and training.

"2. That *all* fatuous children ought to be subjected to the proper means of education in institutions devoted to the purpose.

"3. That such institutions ought to be superintended, or conducted by, properly qualified medical men, who should have the assistance of persons qualified for the task by patience of temper, and by experience of cases more or less similar."

The sum of £500 has lately been set apart by the Ferguson Trustees, to found an Institution for Imbeciles in Glasgow.

Medicine & Society
In America

An Arno Press/New York Times Collection

Alcott, William A. **The Physiology of Marriage.** 1866. New Introduction by Charles E. Rosenberg.

Beard, George M. **American Nervousness:** Its Causes and Consequences. 1881. New Introduction by Charles E. Rosenberg.

Beard, George M. **Sexual Neurasthenia.** 5th edition. 1898.

Beecher, Catharine E. **Letters to the People on Health and Happiness.** 1855.

Blackwell, Elizabeth. **Essays in Medical Sociology.** 1902. Two volumes in one.

Blanton, Wyndham B. **Medicine in Virginia in the Seventeenth Century.** 1930.

Bowditch, Henry I. **Public Hygiene in America.** 1877.

Bowditch, N[athaniel] I. **A History of the Massachusetts General Hospital:** To August 5, 1851. 2nd edition. 1872.

Brill, A. A. **Psychanalysis:** Its Theories and Practical Application. 1913.

Cabot, Richard C. **Social Work:** Essays on the Meeting-Ground of Doctor and Social Worker. 1919.

Cathell, D. W. **The Physician Himself and What He Should Add to His Scientific Acquirements.** 2nd edition. 1882. New Introduction by Charles E. Rosenberg.

The Cholera Bulletin. Conducted by an Association of Physicians. Vol. I: Nos. 1–24. 1832. All published. New Introduction by Charles E. Rosenberg.

Clarke, Edward H. **Sex in Education;** or, A Fair Chance for the Girls. 1873.

Committee on the Costs of Medical Care. **Medical Care for the American People:** The Final Report of The Committee on the Costs of Medical Care, No. 28. [1932].

Currie, William. **An Historical Account of the Climates and Diseases of the United States of America.** 1792.

Davenport, Charles Benedict. **Heredity in Relation to Eugenics.** 1911. New Introduction by Charles E. Rosenberg.

Davis, Michael M. **Paying Your Sickness Bills.** 1931.

Disease and Society in Provincial Massachusetts: Collected Accounts, 1736–1939. 1972.

Earle, Pliny. **The Curability of Insanity:** A Series of Studies. 1887.

Falk, I. S., C. Rufus Rorem, and Martha D. Ring. **The Costs of Medical Care:** A Summary of Investigations on The Economic Aspects of the Prevention and Care of Illness, No. 27. 1933.

Faust, Bernhard C. **Catechism of Health:** For the Use of Schools, and for Domestic Instruction. 1794.

Flexner, Abraham. **Medical Education in the United States and Canada**: A Report to The Carnegie Foundation for the Advancement of Teaching, Bulletin Number Four. 1910.

Gross, Samuel D. **Autobiography of Samuel D. Gross, M.D.**, with Sketches of His Contemporaries. Two volumes. 1887.

Hooker, Worthington. **Physician and Patient**; or, A Practical View of the Mutual Duties, Relations and Interests of the Medical Profession and the Community. 1849.

Howe, S. G. **On the Causes of Idiocy.** 1858.

Jackson, James. **A Memoir of James Jackson, Jr., M.D.** 1835.

Jennings, Samuel K. **The Married Lady's Companion, or Poor Man's Friend.** 2nd edition. 1808.

The Maternal Physician; a Treatise on the Nurture and Management of Infants, from the Birth until Two Years Old. 2nd edition. 1818. New Introduction by Charles E. Rosenberg.

Mathews, Joseph McDowell. **How to Succeed in the Practice of Medicine.** 1905.

McCready, Benjamin W. **On the Influences of Trades, Professions, and Occupations in the United States, in the Production of Disease.** 1943.

Mitchell, S. Weir. **Doctor and Patient.** 1888.

Nichols, T[homas] L. **Esoteric Anthropology: The Mysteries of Man.** [1853].

Origins of Public Health in America: Selected Essays, 1820–1855. 1972.

Osler, Sir William. **The Evolution of Modern Medicine.** 1922.

The Physician and Child-Rearing: Two Guides, 1809–1894. 1972.

Rosen, George. **The Specialization of Medicine**: with Particular Reference to Ophthalmology. 1944.

Royce, Samuel. **Deterioration and Race Education.** 1878.

Rush, Benjamin. **Medical Inquiries and Observations.** Four volumes in two. 4th edition. 1815.

Shattuck, Lemuel, Nathaniel P. Banks, Jr., and Jehiel Abbott. **Report of a General Plan for the Promotion of Public and Personal Health.** Massachusetts Sanitary Commission. 1850.

Smith, Stephen. **Doctor in Medicine** and Other Papers on Professional Subjects. 1872.

Still, Andrew T. **Autobiography of Andrew T. Still**, with a History of the Discovery and Development of the Science of Osteopathy. 1897.

Storer, Horatio Robinson. **The Causation, Course, and Treatment of Reflex Insanity in Women.** 1871.

Sydenstricker, Edgar. **Health and Environment.** 1933.

Thomson, Samuel. **A Narrative, of the Life and Medical Discoveries of Samuel Thomson.** 1822.

Ticknor, Caleb. **The Philosophy of Living**; or, The Way to Enjoy Life and Its Comforts. 1836.

U.S. Sanitary Commission. **The Sanitary Commission of the United States Army**: A Succinct Narrative of Its Works and Purposes. 1864.

White, William A. **The Principles of Mental Hygiene.** 1917.